DORMITION?

DORMITION?

by

Paul Flynn

Creative Christian Publishing

Dormition?

by Paul Flynn

Published 2019 by
Creative Christian Publishing
The Grange, London SW19

english96@msn.com

ISBN 978-0-9539179-8-3

Copyright © 2019 by Paul Flynn

All rights reserved. The author guarantees that all contents are original and do not infringe the rights of any other person or work. No part of this work may be reproduced without the written permission of the author.

Bible quotations are taken either from The New Jerusalem Version, Copyright © 1985 by Darton, Longman & Todd Ltd., or from the King James Version.

ABBREVIATIONS

MD   *Munificentissimus Deus,* the Apostolic Constitution of Venerable Pope Pius XII, November 1, 1950, in which the dogma of the Assumption is defined; quotations from English version on Vatican website.

TTD   *A Treatise on True Devotion to the Blessed Virgin Mary* by St Louis Marie De Montfort. Quoted from the EWTN website.

MMP   *To the Priests, Our Lady's Beloved Sons,* Fr Stefano Gobbi, quotations from the 18th English Edition. References are to the sequential number headings given with each entry in the book.

Note re capitals: The capital in Church is used in referring to the hierarchy and Magisterium of the Church. No capital is used in referring to the church as the entire community of its members.

CONTENTS

FOREWARD

WHAT DOES THE ASSUMPTION MEAN?

WHAT DIFFERENCE DOES IT MAKE FOR US?

THE QUESTION

WHO DID IT?

A NATURAL DEATH?

DID SHE DIE VOLUNTARILY?

EARLY CENTURIES

ST EPIPHANIUS

500-1000 A.D.

1000-1850 A.D.

AFTER 1854

THE ROSARY

RESURRECTION VERSUS ASSUMPTION

ENOCH, MOSES

ELIJAH

THE SHULAMITE IN THE SONG OF SONGS

THE MARIAN DOCTRINES IN THE SONG OF SONGS

THE DORMITION IN THE SONG OF SONGS?

IN THE MOMENTS BEFORE THE ASSUMPTION

THE ENMITY

THE APPARITIONS and REVELATION 12

THE CHURCH OF ROME

THE THREE ASCENTS

MATURING IN PRAISE

CONCLUSION

FOREWORD

The Church teaches as part of the faith that at the end of her earthly life Mary was taken up body and soul into heaven. The Assumption is what we call a dogma of the faith, something which Christians must believe if they are to hold to the faith handed on by the apostles in its integrity.

Some Christians believe that she was taken up without ever dying. Others believe that she died and remained dead for a short time, a couple of days or so, and was assumed into heaven by her Son before her flesh had begun to decay. In other words, they believe in the Dormition of Mary. The term Dormition, as used by those who believe in it, includes the idea of the Assumption.

As to whether she died first, the Church leaves us free to believe either way. We are required to believe that she was assumed into heaven before her flesh decayed. Whether she died first is an open question. We can take one side or the other without thereby falling into heresy.

In this little work I explore the question, whether Mary died, from as many angles as I can think of. I should admit at the outset that I am of the view that Mary was taken up while still alive, that she didn't die. I take this view strongly but without absolute certainty. There are good arguments against it and I will be as respectful and objective as I can in dealing with each aspect of the issue, remembering that some of the greatest and holiest minds in church history, very many of whom have been exemplary in their devotion to the Mother of God, have taken the opposite view to mine.

Apart from chapters on miscellaneous topics, there are three principal strands in the thoughts I put forward in this work.

1. I take an unprofessional look at the phases of the history of the doctrine of the Assumption and of the Dormition, to see if any trends can be picked out that might point us to one answer or the other. I find a development, from the first centuries of church history in which questions about the end of Mary's life seemed to be of no interest to the church at all; to a period of widespread interest in the Dormition of Mary, her death and her being taken up to heaven by the Lord; to a period in which the taking up, or Assumption gradually emerged as the most significant element in the account of the end of her life; to a period of belief, principally among lay Christians of the western Catholic church, beginning sometime before 1500 and growing since that time, that she was assumed without having died.

2. I take a serious look at the question, Who did it? Who was the agent of death in Mary's case if she did indeed die? The answer frequently offered to this question is that no one did it, she just died a 'natural' death as we all do, and as plants and animals do. This answer is subjected to critical scrutiny in the light of relevant Scripture.

3. Considerable attention is given in these pages to a very common question - Where in the Bible does it say that Mary was assumed? In seeking an answer to this question I've been surprised to find that not alone is Mary's Assumption referred to in Scripture. It is vividly described, and its setting is described too. They are described prophetically in beautiful images and allusions, and a lot of detail is missing, but the moments in which the Assumption of Mary happened are indeed described. And the description seems to indicate clearly that she did not die before being assumed. My hope for this short work is that one of its principal takeaways will be that the question - Where in the Bible does it say that she was assumed? - will become redundant.

In case anyone is offended at anything I say, please let me make it clear that I am not writing this work in any official ecclesial capacity. I am a lay Catholic Christian, have not been appointed by the Church to write this work, and am far from being qualified to write a professional work of theology on any subject. It is offered as nothing more than an individual believer's attempt to explore an issue that engages some Christians.

WHAT DOES THE ASSUMPTION MEAN?

When the body has been resurrected, it is not the same as it was before. It is recognizable as the body of the same person, but it has taken on altogether enhanced powers.

Jesus was recognized by his disciples when he came among them after his Resurrection, though not always immediately, because his body exercised greater powers. He could enter a room while the doors were locked. He could multilocate. He could give himself Eucharistically, as he did at Emmaus, when the disciples at last 'recognized him in the breaking of bread' (Luke 24:35).

As St Paul explained:

> What you sow is not the body that is to be, but only a bare grain, of wheat I dare say ...
> - 1 Corinthians 15:37

Paul is here using the same image Jesus used.

> Truly I say to you, unless a grain of wheat falls into the earth and dies, it remains only a single grain, but if it dies it will bear much fruit.   - John 12:24

The point here is that something happens at the resurrection of our bodies to make us very different from before. And this was true even of Jesus. He could have exercised the power of his divinity before his Resurrection. Sometimes he did, in his miracles, for example, and in his Transfiguration. Normally, however, the body he walked around in before his death was like ours, vulnerable, capable of being done to death, limited in time and space.

> What is sown is perishable, what is raised is imperishable ... what is sown is weak, what is raised is powerful; what is sown is a natural body, what is raised is a spiritual body.   - 1 Corinthians 15:42-44

This is the key point: The earthly body is not 'spiritual,' meaning it is not normally enjoying the full experience of the presence of God. Such experience would be too much for our earthly flesh to bear. As Scripture says, 'No man can see God and live' (Exodus 33:20).

On this earth we are in a time of testing. God hides himself from us and we can only know him by faith, which is exceedingly pleasing to him. Later, after our resurrection, we come into the presence of God in a spiritualized body, a body fully adapted for the glorious presence of God and the powers which can be exercised because of that presence. Those powers are beyond anything we can imagine now.

> What I am saying brothers is that mere flesh and blood cannot inherit the kingdom of God; what is perishable cannot inherit what is imperishable ... we are all going to be changed instantly, in the twinkling of an eye, when the last trumpet sounds, and we will be changed because this perishable nature of ours must put on imperishability, this mortal nature must put on immortality.
> - 1 Corinthians 15:50-53

Mary was assumed into heaven long before we will be resurrected and taken up. She was assumed when her earthly life came to an end.

Her Assumption was a great privilege given to her by her Son, but it was not given to her for her own sake alone. It was given to her also to equip her for what she was to do as Queen and Mother of the church.

What her Assumption means for us is that she can now care for the entire church throughout the earth and until the close of the age with a human Heart, a Heart of flesh, a Heart which has been enlarged with all the powers of a resurrected body to be in all places at all times.

In her case it happened 'in the twinkling of an eye,' at the end of her earthly life. She did not need to wait until the end as we do, because God determined that she should be with us in all the fullness of her resurrection power bodily, from the earliest beginnings of the church's life to the end.

The church still struggling on earth has this great source of strength and confidence. We look to her not as a disembodied soul marked by the wages of sin. We look to her as totally victorious over the devil and all his works, and we are powerfully encouraged in doing so. We look to her knowing that she cares for us with all the power of her glorified body; knowing that she is present to us with a Heart of flesh and blood; knowing that the devil and his wicked angels are terrified of her because of the completeness of her victory over them.

Her Assumption is a defined dogma of the Church. There is no doubt about it and we are not concerned in this work to argue about it. The issue in this book is whether Mary died before she was assumed.

It is sometimes said that it doesn't matter whether she died or not, because the effect of her Assumption is the same either way.

I don't agree that it doesn't matter. Whether she died or not is a question that can and should be asked because it concerns the extent of her victory over Satan and his wicked angels.

One could argue that because the 'spiritualized' body in heaven is so different from the body on earth, there needs to be a clean break between the two states, the earthly and the heavenly, and that death is necessary to accomplish that clean break.

St Paul's reference to 'the twinkling of an eye' is helpful in this respect. God can change us from an earthly body to a spiritualized body fit for heaven in a single instant if he wants to, and in fact when St Paul uses the phrase he is speaking of those who are to be saved and are still alive at the Second Coming. Their bodies, being still on earth, will make the transition from the earthly state to the heavenly state 'in the twinkling of an eye.'

It would therefore not be true to say that Mary needed to go through death in order to make the transition from the earthly to the heavenly state.

If one accepts the account of Fr Gobbi of the Marian Movement of Priests, the 'twinkling of an eye' is an accurate description of the suddenness with which Mary made the transition. Among the things Fr Gobbi reports Mary as saying to him is this, recorded for the Feast of the Assumption, 1996:

> "Your heavenly Mother was assumed into heaven at the very moment when she closed her eyes to her earthly life."   - MMP 576

This very brief statement of her Assumption deals with our point with great economy of words. She recognizes that there was a moment which divided what went before from what came next. She acknowledges that there was a great difference between her earthly life and her heavenly life. The Assumption was not a seamless move from one place and state to the other as though she entered heaven with a body unchanged from the one she had during her earthly life. She only says that the transition happened in a single moment, or 'in the twinkling of an eye' as St Paul put it.

WHAT DIFFERENCE DOES IT MAKE FOR US?

Before we address the question whether Mary died first, we will consider what impact her Assumption has on us. Why do we need Mary in her glorified body? Couldn't we pray to her as we pray to the other saints? Couldn't she give us the protection we need her to give us as a disembodied spirit waiting in heaven to be reunited with her body, as the other saints are?

As Mary has been given maternal authority over Christ our head, she has also been given maternal authority over us, his body, his Bride the church on earth.

It is the desire of our Savior that his Mother and ours be united with him by being engaged in the work of our salvation as intimately as he is.

She could not fulfill this commission as a disembodied spirit, marked by the defeat gained over us by Satan.

She fulfills this commission in glory, having been assumed body and soul into heaven.

The role Mary is called to play in bringing her errant children back to union with their divine Savior is necessary for our salvation. We are saved by the Blood of Jesus. But we are not united with Jesus by being isolated from his Mother and ours.

> Draw me after you, let us run.
> The king has brought me into his chambers;
> you will be our joy and our gladness.
> - Song of Songs 1:4

The switches from singular pronouns to plural tell the tale. Mary enters into union with God first; we his church follow her.

Jesus has a passionate desire, which he will not set aside, for his Bride the church to enter into deep, intimate and complete union with his Mother and only in this way to enter into deep, intimate and complete union with himself.

> Ah, why are you not my brother,
> nursed at the breast of my mother!
> - Song of Songs 8:1

Why does he cry out for this to happen? What difference does it make to him? He explains in the same verse:

> Then I could kiss you abroad
> and I would not be despised.
> - Song of Songs 8:1

We can go to Jesus direct in our prayer. We can bypass Mary for a time. If we take this route, however, we will soon get into trouble, and the trouble will be serious. We begin to take God too casually. We begin to take liberties. We take the blessings we receive in prayer as a congratulatory message from the Most High, and we fall into spiritual pride. Our flesh and our emotions rejoice in the spiritual intimacy we enjoy with the Lord and our prayer becomes unclean, even as we are congratulating ourselves about it. We lose holy fear.

The result of all this is that God cannot continue to support our prayer life. We lose the ability to pray. We lose all sense of his presence. We become convinced he has rejected us, and like Saul visiting the witch of Endor (1 Samuel 28), we turn for comfort and support to other spiritual entities; we engage with the occult. We praise spirits whom Christian believers praise at their mortal peril.

Whole communities in the church get themselves into a terrible mess in these ways. The worst and most embarrassing evils follow.

In the midst of this mess, Jesus cries out his appeal to us. Why have you forgotten what I've told you? Why will you not take the remedy I've given you? Why will you not become my brother by allowing yourself to be nurtured by my mother? In a short time she will unmask the horrible errors you have fallen into. You will be able truly to repent of your sins and she will lead you back to intimate union with me, with no need for me to be embarrassed at my Bride the church because she has abused her privileges.

Jesus says:

> "I would lead you,
> I would bring you into my mother's house."
> - Song of Songs 8:2

The church replies:

> "And she would instruct me!"
> - Song of Songs 8:2

Mary agrees:

> "I would cause you to drink of spiced wine,
> the juice of my pomegranates."
> - Song of Songs 8:2

Mary brings us the grace of God with a strength that is unique, a 'spiced' mixture that is so potent against the wiles of our enemy the devil that he will have no choice but to run away from us. Where Mary is present, all demons are compelled to leave.

Why does Jesus ask us to approach him through Mary? Why will he only give us his best gifts if we consecrate ourselves to her? Can he not deal with us directly?

He can. He is sovereign and he is almighty. He can do anything.

But when God chose Mary to be his Mother, he also committed himself to honor her in accordance with his own commandment, 'Honor your father and your mother.'

He will not ignore his Mother in dealing with his people, his church. He will not forget that he was taken from one of us, from one of the children of Adam, related by blood to the entire human race. He has appointed her as Queen of his kingdom and Mother of his church, and he has given her all the gifts she needs to carry out her role with total efficacy.

He has prepared her for this by taking her up to glory with himself, body and soul.

We are not led by a defeated Mother.

We are not led by a Queen who is marked by the victory Satan gained over the race of Adam.

We are led by a Mother already glorified with her Son.

That is why the Assumption of Mary is so important for us. That is why it has been defined as part of our faith, and we cannot hold the Christian faith in its integrity without believing it. Only the Queen assumed body and soul into heaven can fulfill the commission in our regard given to her by her Son.

THE QUESTION

Our question arises fairly frequently in Christian forums and blogs: Did Mary die before she was taken up? The question typically comes from a young person who always understood that her Assumption meant that she was taken up without experiencing death, and who dislikes having to revise this view on learning that, historically, the majority of notable churchmen have taken the view that she died first.

Romans 6:23 – 'The wages of sin is death,' is usually cited as compelling support for the belief that Mary, being wholly without sin, was free of any need to pay the wages of sin and therefore did not have to die.

The forum or blog host deals with the enquirer sympathetically and assures him that he is free to continue believing that Mary was assumed while still alive, but with hints that he might need to mature a little further in his thinking as he did when he learned the truth about Santa Claus, for example.

My sympathy when I see these enquiries is always with the enquirer. The enquirer is motivated, in my opinion, by a godly desire, which is the desire to praise Mary as highly as a creature can possible be praised. God himself praises Mary so lavishly, and he does it publicly, in his word, that it cannot be wrong for Christians to take inspiration from this and to desire to praise God's greatest creature as lavishly as God himself praises her.

Are we sure we are right in asking our fellow Christians to reduce the praises they give to Mary? Admittedly, most of the churchmen who ever discussed the issue came down firmly in favor of the belief that Mary died before she was assumed; but are we sure we are not quenching the spirit when we discourage those who wish to praise Mary as highly as they possibly can?

Whether one believes in the Dormition of Mary can depend on the account one received when first taught about her Assumption.

The Fathers generally understood that she died in the usual course of events, and her body was placed in a tomb, but before her flesh had time to begin to decay she was resurrected and assumed body and soul into heaven by her Divine Son. Mary's Dormition, her brief falling asleep, was integral to the concept they had of her Assumption. In the Orthodox and Eastern Catholic churches I understand that when they celebrate the Assumption they refer to it as the Dormition, each term implying the other, so inseparably interwoven are the two concepts in their understanding.

I had the opposite experience. When as a child I learned about Mary's Assumption, my parents and teachers left me in no doubt that she was taken up while still alive. That she did not die was part and parcel of the understanding I was given of her Assumption.

It took a long time before the thought even entered my mind that she might have died. I was past the age of thirty when a group of people I was in conversation with asked me what I thought. Did she die before she was taken up? These were people I respected, and I was taken aback that they could even think of asking a question that appeared nonsensical to me.

"If she died before she was taken up," I replied with total certainty in what I was saying, "the Church would have to teach the resurrection of Mary before it could speak about her Assumption. I never heard that the Church teaches as doctrine that Mary was resurrected. Did you?"

They all nodded agreement, and the subject was immediately changed.

Much later, I was again surprised to learn that the opinion that Mary died first, before she was assumed, is far from being an eccentric one. The overwhelming majority of the Fathers, saints, doctors of the church, and popes who expressed a view on the subject were convinced that Mary first died and was resurrected, then was taken up to heaven by Jesus. The overwhelming weight of theological opinion was that she died and remained dead for a short time before being taken up.

I had to learn late that, while it is permissible to take either side in the argument, it is not permissible for either side to impugn the other. Did anyone ever speak more affectingly of the Mother of God than St Alphonsus Liguori? Was anyone as eloquent or as effective in moving the hearts of sinners to take refuge in her intercession? If a man as saintly as St Alphonsus Liguori took the view that Mary died before she was assumed, that is proof that it is a reputable and even a holy view to take.

WHO DID IT?

At the heart of many people's internal protest at the idea of the 'death' of Mary there is a question. If this question cannot be satisfactorily answered, the credibility of the 'death' of Mary cannot be satisfactorily established.

Here is the question: If Mary died, which destroyer did God release against her? Who was the agent of her death?

Did she kill herself? Perish the thought.

Did God kill her? Of course not. God is never the agent of death. He permits it. Because of sin he releases the agent of death against us, but he is not himself the agent of death. This is very clear in Scripture.

> For death is not of God's fashioning,
> ... but the godless call for death in deed and word.
> - Wisdom 1:13-16

We know that Jesus did not have to die. He laid down his life voluntarily, suffering death at the hands of lawless and demonized men. Did Mary follow him in this? Did she suffer a violent death at the hands of demonized men? There is no evidence of that, and I have never heard anyone claiming that it happened, so it can be reasonably discounted.

It is frequently argued that Mary died in the ordinary course of nature, just like everyone else, and just like plants and animals, which are also without sin and yet are destined for death. I believe this argument cannot be sustained against a reading of the relevant scriptures, and I will address this issue and cite these scriptures in the chapter after this one.

So who was the agent of death in Mary's case, if indeed she did die? There can only be one answer to this question, and it is given in Scripture.

> Death came into the world through the devil's envy.
> - Wisdom 2:24

'For this purpose the Son of God was manifested, that he might destroy the works of the devil' (1 John 3:8). The works of the devil are sin, and death, and all manner of suffering.

Death is the work of the devil.

Excepting those who are alive at the Second Coming, the devil will gain one victory over all of us, even if we have been sanctified when the time of our death comes. Death will be swallowed up in victory because of the victorious Cross of Christ, but we will have to endure the humiliation of defeat once. We will have to die at the hands of our Adversary, Satan and his wicked angels.

Did Mary endure death at the hands of Satan and his wicked angels?

I don't believe she did. It would surprise me greatly if Jesus did not spare her this indignity.

The enmity between Mary and the devil is spelt out at the beginning of Scripture in Genesis, and at the end in Revelation. This ancient enmity runs very deep. Mary is inveterately hostile to the devil and all his works. She will not hesitate to crush his head with her heel even as he watches his opportunity against all her children.

Mary was never overpowered by the devil and his angels. He tried every trick in his book to bring her down, just as he did against Jesus. But he never succeeded. Like Jesus, she dismissed all of his filthy approaches through her humble and total dependence on her God and the constant attention she gave to his word.

Satan could find no way to breach her defences. He has no way in where someone is so immersed in the word of God that, as Jesus did when he was tempted in the desert, she draws forth the scripture which is specifically designed in every case to beat off the devil's attack.

Mary was never overpowered by the devil. It strikes me as wholly discordant if it were found that Jesus allowed Satan to gain one big victory over her by doing her to death. He was allowed to accomplish the death of Jesus for a specific purpose. Jesus suffered death only to overcome it forever for all of us.

Mary helped him to accomplish it. She was present at every step of the Way of the Cross, and she suffered in her Son's death far more than she would ever have suffered in her own death, if she did indeed die. Her own death would have added nothing to the death she died when the sword of sorrow pierced her heart underneath the Cross at Calvary.

Jesus gained the victory at Calvary. He vanquished death once and for all. Jesus is the warrior, the Lion of the Tribe of Judah whose victory is forever, whose kingship will never come to an end.

Mary his Mother was with him through every moment of the warfare. She was a victim of every stroke of the lash, every piercing of the nails, every buffet, every fall into the dirt and the blood, every hammering of the nails into his flesh.

Jesus asked her to suffer with him in all his suffering, but he did not ask his Mother to submit her own flesh and her own skin and her own blood and her own life to the devil. It would, in my view, have been inappropriate to do so.

But why, it might be asked, if God allowed Mary to be tempted by the devil as Jesus was, did he not allow her to be tested by the experience of death as Jesus was? If she suffered the indignity of being assailed by the devil's temptations, why not the indignity of death?

By the testing of temptation the devil aims to induce us to evil by committing sin. Temptation can lead to evil, but temptation is not itself evil. When we succeed in rejecting temptation the result is most pleasing to God. The devil and his angels will approach us from every angle trying to bring us down. They will try to exploit every weakness. They will try to lead us into every sin. They will try to trick us into acting against every word that has proceeded out of the mouth of God.

But as long as we rely on the strength and the word of our God to resist, the devil and his angels fail. They have tried to accomplish evil, and have failed. No evil has touched us as long as the Lord comes to our help and we refuse to take the bait.

Death, by contrast, is an accomplished evil.

Death is not to be compared with sin, which is an offence committed rather than an offence suffered. Still, death is a victory of the enemy in which the enemy exults and rejoices. That is why I believe Mary was not subject to death and did not in fact die.

If I am correct in this, then we are left with the answer to our question by process of elimination.

If Mary died, who was the agent of death? No one. There was no agent of death. No destroyer was released against her by God. The reason is, I believe, that she didn't die. We will now consider the question of whether she died a 'natural' death.

A NATURAL DEATH?

Is it right to speak of death as 'natural'?

It can sound right to our ears. Plants and animals are destined to die naturally. They are without sin, and yet they die. So why not human beings?

I would be careful with this argument. Death in the case of plants and animals is not the same thing as death in the case of humans.

Plants and animals are made for man. We are allowed by God to treat them as our property and as our food.

> And God said, Let us make man in our own image and in our own likeness, and let them have dominion over the fish of the sea, and over the birds of the air, and over the cattle, and all the animals and the creatures that creep along the ground.   - Genesis 1:26

Death is indeed therefore the natural destiny of plants and animals. They are in our ownership and they are at our service. We have a right to decide which ones to farm for food, which ones to weed out, which ones to cultivate.

Death is not the natural destiny of humans.

> For God created human beings to be immortal,
> he made them as an image of his own eternity;
> death came into the world through the devil's envy,
> as those who belong to him find to their cost.
>
> — Wisdom 2:23,24

If man had never sinned, we would all have finished our time of testing on this earth not by dying, but by being taken up victoriously to glory in heaven. This is what happened to Enoch (see Hebrews 11:5, Genesis 5:24) and Elijah (see 2 Kings 2).

Does Scripture teach unambiguously that we humans would not have had to die if we had not sinned? If we can establish this point from Scripture, then the argument that Mary died 'in the ordinary course of nature' is clearly invalidated.

I believe the point can be established from Scripture. There are a number of scriptures which, taken together, seem to place the issue beyond any doubt. They occur in the early chapters of Genesis in which the original state of our first parents, before they sinned, is described. The context is set in this passage:

> And out of the ground the Lord God made every good tree to grow that is pleasant to the sight and good for food, with the tree of life in the middle of the garden, and the tree of the knowledge of good and evil.
>
> - Genesis 2:9

These two trees stood in the middle of the garden, not far from each other. It was very easy for Adam and Eve to pluck the fruit of either of them and eat it.

God, however, issued a command:

> Then Yahweh God gave the man this command: "Of every tree in the garden you may freely eat; but of the tree of the knowledge of good and evil you must not eat, for on the day you eat of it you will surely die."
>
> - Genesis 2:16,17

This command is framed positively. They were to be wholly free to eat of all the trees of the garden with only one exception, the tree of the knowledge of good and evil. The command makes it clear that they were to be wholly free to eat from the tree of life, at that stage, because the tree of the knowledge of good and evil is the only tree whose fruit Adam and Eve were forbidden to eat.

We know what happened after this. The serpent tempted Eve with the fruit of the forbidden tree. He told her it would make her like God, knowing good from evil. Eve ate of the fruit of the forbidden tree and gave it to Adam, who also ate of it.

Once they did this, their condition changed radically. Before they ate of the forbidden fruit they were wholly innocent, wholly free of sin. They were 'naked and were not ashamed,' being free of any hint of anything offensive to God. Consequently, they were in no way subject to the results of sin. They were not subject to suffering and death, and the fruit of the tree of life was there for them to eat at any time. All they had to do, if they wanted to live forever, was to pluck the fruit of the tree of life and to eat it.

The following passage tells us with great precision what changed as a result of their sin. It describes the new situation of Adam and Eve after they had sinned, and it goes right to the heart of the matter. The result of their sin was that Adam and Eve were banished from the original state of immortality in which God had placed them. They were cut off from access to the tree of life. They were no longer able to eat of its fruit and so to live forever.

Then Yahweh God said, "Behold, the man has become as one of us, knowing good and evil; he must not be allowed to reach out his hand and pick from the tree of life too, and eat and live forever." Therefore the Lord God sent him out from the garden of Eden to till the ground from which he had been taken. He drove out the man, and in front of the garden of Eden he posted the great winged creatures and the fiery flashing sword, to guard the way to the tree of life.

- Genesis 3:22-24

We know that the tree of life was in the garden before they sinned. We've seen in Genesis 2:9 that the tree of life stood in the middle of the garden, alongside the tree of the knowledge of good and evil. Adam and Eve were expelled from the garden to prevent them from ever reaching out and picking the fruit of the tree of life.

The key thing to note here is that Adam and Eve were not cut off from access to the tree of life before they sinned; on the contrary, they were commanded to eat freely of it; they were only cut off from access to it afterwards.

In other words, immortality was taken away from Adam and Eve only after they had sinned. Before they sinned they were not destined to die, not even by a 'natural' death.

I consider this to be clear scriptural proof that death is the result of sin for us humans, and where there is no sin, there is no subjection to death. The Holy Spirit meant exactly what he said through St Paul when he taught us that, 'The wages of sin is death' (Romans 6:23).

We humans were not destined by God to die when he created us. Our liability to death is a result only of sin. In our case, unlike the case of plants and animals, which are there for our use and consumption, death is not our 'natural' destiny.

This is why the argument that Mary died a 'natural' death is flawed. It is unscriptural. Her Immaculate Conception and her freedom from any actual sin rendered her completely free from the common lot of sinful humanity; she was completely free from death.

But, it is sometimes argued, the death of Christ, which he undertook voluntarily, has given death a different meaning and a positive value, and for this reason the claim that Mary died does not deprive her of her privileges or of the respect due to her on account of her total innocence. It is simply an affirmation that she followed her Son all the way, taking a free decision to accept her own personal death in imitation of him, as all the members of his kingdom are called to do.

This argument finds considerable scriptural support and I therefore regard it as one of the most powerful arguments in favor of the Dormition of Mary. I will address it in the next chapter.

DID SHE DIE VOLUNTARILY?

None of the New Testament saints after Mary have been taken up as Enoch and Elijah were. Does this mean that Enoch and Elijah achieved a greater state of holiness than any of the New Testament saints? The answer to this has to be no. Jesus said that no man has ever arisen greater than St John the Baptist, and yet the least in the kingdom of heaven which he, Jesus, was establishing is greater than St John the Baptist (Matthew 11:11).

So how can it be that the two Old Testament figures, Enoch and Elijah, were assumed into heaven, but no New Testament saint after Mary was assumed?

The answer is that the death of Jesus, by which we have all been redeemed and saved, has given the death of all of us a priceless value. He has made our death the means by which we are united to him.

> Precious in the eyes of the Lord
> is the death of his faithful.
> - Psalm 116:15

> "Blessed are the dead who die in the Lord henceforth."
> - Revelation 14:13

St Paul explains more exactly why the death of a disciple is so precious.

> If we have been joined to him in a death like his, so we shall be in a resurrection like his.
>
> - Romans 6:5

Our death becomes the means of our being 'joined' to Christ, or 'planted' together with him. If we allow him to die in us, our death opens us to his power to save us. If we accept our death in union with his death, he will share his Resurrection with us too. And it will not only benefit us; it will contribute to 'fill up the measure of Christ's sufferings for the sake of his body the church' (Colossians 1:24). The church, being the body of Christ the Head, suffers with him for the salvation of the world.

If our death, united to the death of Christ, is so precious, so powerful to save us his church, why would we wish to deny the same privilege to Mary? Is it not right to admit that Mary died out of a desire to unite herself to her Son in a death like his so that he would share his Resurrection with her and with the rest of his church? Why would Mary be the sole exception to the rule, that he joins us to his Resurrection after we have been joined to his death?

There is serious force in this argument. Many of the Fathers were convinced by it, and declared that Mary accepted death voluntarily at the request of Jesus in order to do what we are all called to do, to be united with him in a death like his so that he will unite us to him in his Resurrection.

And in one sense it is true. It is true that Mary united herself with Jesus in a death like his. The difference in Mary's case is that the death she died was not her own personal death, it was the death of her Son Jesus.

Mary did not endure Simeon's Sword of Sorrow by herself dying. Her own death would have been a very easy matter compared to what she went through at her Son's Crucifixion. She experienced the Sword of Sorrow by following her Son every step of the way to Calvary, and seeing him draw his last breath there. No death that Mary could have endured would have been anything like as painful as the death she died with Jesus on Calvary.

This was prophesied in the Song of Songs. Mary, the Bride, loses track of the Groom. She goes out into the streets of Jerusalem looking for him. She meets the watchmen who stand guard on the walls and police the city. Then this happens:

> The watchmen met me,
>
> those who go on their rounds in the city.
>
> They beat me, they wounded me,
>
> they took away my mantle,
>
> those guardians of the walls!
>
> - Song of Songs 5:7

This is a condensed description of the Passion of Our Lord, yet Mary is prophetically shown describing it here not as happening to him but as happening to her. She is prophetically shown here suffering every part of his Way of the Cross, and enduring every moment of his Crucifixion on Calvary.

Mary was so intimately and personally united with her Son in his death, that her own death would have added nothing to the Sword of Sorrow she experienced on Calvary. That is why I believe that Mary, alone among the figures of the New Testament, alone among the members of the church, was not called upon to undergo a separate death of her own. She entered into Jesus' Resurrection not by herself dying, but by uniting herself with the death of Jesus so intimately that she experienced his death as something far worse than her own 'death' could ever have been.

As a Doctor of the Church, St Louis Marie De Montfort expressed it:

> 'Even at his death she had to be present so that he might be united with her in one sacrifice and be immolated with her consent to the eternal Father.'
>
> - TTD (10)

Mary's union with her Son in his sacrificial death is very mysterious, wholly different from the union we reach with him by way of our own death. She was united with him 'in one sacrifice,' and he was offered to the Father 'with her consent.' This means that any talk of Mary achieving union with the death of Jesus by means of a death of her own seems out of place. She had already achieved union with the death of Jesus.

EARLY CENTURIES

The development of doctrine in regard to Mary was very gradual and a little complicated. In the first five centuries or so of its history, the Church's primary concern was to clarify the teachings in regard to Christ our Savior. The great Marian doctrines were secondary to this concern.

On the other hand, because our understanding of Christ and his Incarnation is so intimately bound up with our understanding of the role and person of Mary, some of the Marian doctrines were well understood from the beginning. The doctrine of the Virgin Birth is indicated in Luke's gospel and was understood and accepted from the earliest centuries of Church history.

That Mary is the Mother of God was defined as a doctrine of the faith at the Council of Ephesus in the year 431 A.D. This doctrine means that a human being, a child of Adam, of the line of Abraham, has been found so profoundly holy, so profoundly submitted to God as to be worthy to be given authority over him. The definition of Mary Mother God established the truth that Mary is incomparably the greatest creature that God has ever made.

That Mary was sinless was understood from the beginning. However, what was understood was that Mary never committed actual sin. The doctrine of the Immaculate Conception, the teaching that from the beginning of her existence she was preserved by God free from contracting any trace of the original sin of Adam and Eve, developed much later and was not defined as dogma until 1854.

The two doctrines, the doctrine of the Immaculate Conception and the doctrine of the Assumption, are closely bound up with each other. In the document *Munificentissimus Deus,* in which Pope Pius XII defined the doctrine of the Assumption in 1950, he declared:

'These two privileges *(Mary's Immaculate Conception and her Assumption)* are most closely bound to one another.' - MD 4

The reason Mary's most holy body was glorified without seeing corruption is that she was wholly without any trace of sin, not even the mark of original sin which we all inherit from Adam.

We can see from the comment of Pope Pius XII that one very important reason the Church in the earliest centuries did not have a fully clarified doctrine of the Assumption is that it did not have a fully clarified doctrine of the Immaculate Conception.

There are other reasons. In those early centuries the Church was engaged in struggles to establish itself and to defend the teachings of the apostles against a great variety of heresies. Some of these heresies related to Mary.

There were sects which sought to glorify Mary in wrongheaded ways, treating her as a goddess and setting up orders of priestesses to offer sacrifice to her. It became necessary to correct such ideas and make it clear that while the Mother of the Lord is highly honored by God, she has all her great gifts from God and not from herself. She is therefore to be highly praised and venerated as the greatest masterpiece of all God's works, but she is not to be worshiped as a goddess.

In ancient pagan Rome, the gods were called the 'immortal' gods. Immortality and divinity went hand in hand. This provides a clue to another difficulty the early Church would have had with promoting a doctrine of the Assumption. It would have led people to refer to Mary as 'immortal,' and so people could easily have become confused and lined her up as one of the pagan goddesses of Rome, which would of course be an abomination. Any talk of Mary's Assumption could quickly have degenerated into serious misunderstanding.

Compounding matters further was the struggle the early Church had with heretical teachings that Jesus was not really human, that he was not really flesh and blood like the rest of us, but only appeared to be.

As early as in the letters of St John the apostle we see this concern to make it clear that Jesus was a real flesh and blood man. The 'test of spirits' in 1 John 4:1-3 is that the good spirits, who are of God, confess that Jesus Christ 'has come in the flesh.' The sinister spirits, who are of the devil, do not confess that Jesus has come in the flesh. If they can fool us into denying that he has come in the flesh, they can also persuade us that he didn't really die, he only appeared to die. And if he didn't really die, he didn't really rise again, he only appeared to rise again.

If Jesus didn't die, we are not saved from our sins. If Jesus didn't rise from the dead, our faith is in vain (1 Corinthians 15:17).

That is why it was so important in those early centuries to avoid promoting the idea that Mary was an 'immortal goddess.' It was important to emphasize that she was a humble, ordinary human being like us. It was not the right time for the doctrine of the Assumption. That would have sent out very confusing signals.

The Marian doctrines developed gradually, and with good reason. Writing in the year 1712, St Louis Marie De Montfort, the great prophet of the growth in the recognition of Mary's role in the modern church, explained the gradualness of their development thus:

'Mary scarcely appeared in the first coming of Jesus Christ so that men, as yet insufficiently instructed and enlightened concerning the Person of her Son, might not wander from the truth by becoming too strongly attached to her. This apparently would have happened if she had been known, on account of the wondrous charms with which Almighty God had endowed even her outward appearance. So true is this that St Denis the Areopagite tells us in his writings that when he saw her, he would have taken her as a goddess because of her incomparable beauty had not his well grounded faith taught him otherwise. But in the Second Coming of Jesus Christ, Mary must be known and openly revealed by the Holy Spirit so that Jesus may be known, loved and served through her. The reasons that moved the Holy Spirit to hide his spouse during her life and to reveal but very little of her since the first teaching of the gospel exist no longer.'   - TTD 49

This helps us to understand the context of the earliest written discourse on Mary's Assumption, which was conducted anonymously and with emphasis on her Dormition. To avoid setting her up as a 'goddess' it was seen as important to state that she died before she was taken up.

In the surviving records of the first three centuries of the Church's history, the Assumption is not mentioned at all. Origen (184-253 A.D.) mentioned Mary's death, but without any indication of her Assumption.

The earliest surviving written work treating of her Dormition and Assumption is a book from around the year 300 A.D., published anonymously, called the *Liber Requiei Mariae,* the *Book of the Repose of Mary.* This book was summarized and further adapted in a book of the late 300s, the *Transitus Mariae,* or *The Passing of Mary,* by an author using the name of St Melitus of Sardis. The *Transitus Mariae* was rejected as apocryphal by Pope Gelasius I in 494 A.D.

These earliest written accounts of Mary's Dormition and Assumption were not such as to inspire a high degree of confidence in the doctrine. They were written anonymously or under pseudonyms, suggesting that the authors themselves feared that their works would come under condemnation.

They were expressed in stories with magical elements, making it still more difficult to take them seriously either as factual records or as expressions of true doctrine.

They placed high emphasis on the death of Mary prior to her Assumption, and the presence at her death of all the apostles, two elements that might have helped them to win acceptance. They did not win acceptance initially, however. They were rejected by Church authorities.

The rejection of these two works is understandable, because they seem to have arisen out of thin air. There are no earlier written records making anything like the claims they make. It is possible that these two works gave expression to a belief already well established, but there is no evidence of this. It is also possible that they provided the early impetus for belief in the Dormition and Assumption to gain a foothold among the faithful.

It would probably be closest to the truth to suggest that they gave expression to a widespread desire among the faithful to have a fitting and reliable record of what happened to Mary at the end of her life, a record with which they could confidently give her the honor appropriate to her. This is about the most convincing explanation we can come up with for their popularity among the Christians of the 300s and 400s.

The desire for such a reliable record had to remain unsatisfied for several centuries. In the absence of definitive teaching on the subject, a wish for true doctrine about the end of Mary's life was all that was available.

The earliest senior churchman to write anything noteworthy about the Assumption using his own name was St Epiphanius. We will take a look at what he said in the next chapter.

ST EPIPHANIUS

St Epiphanius (322-403 A.D.), the saintly bishop of Cyprus, was one of the great fighters against heresy of his era. He wrote a long work called the *Panarion,* meaning 'medicine chest,' (of remedies against heresies, later renamed *Adversus Haereses, 'Against the Heresies'*). It was divided into three books written between 374 and 377 A.D. In this work he argued against a vast collection of heresies, all the ones he knew of.

His style was feisty and irascible, and he was not especially sensitive to the feelings of those whose teachings he attacked. The *Panarion* nevertheless provides a highly informative scan of the thought strands circulating and threatening the faith of Christians in the late 300s. To some extent one needs to read between the lines to see what the problem was, because he wasted no time characterizing each heresy. He paid them no such honor. His only concern was to drive them away by bringing the light of Gospel truth to bear against them.

In a few passages of his work against the heresies and idolatrous practices concerning Mary, we can gain an invaluable glimpse of the state of thinking of a conscientious churchman of the late 300s in her regard. We will take a look at three of his comments here, all of them from near the end of Book 2 of the *Panarion*.

The first appears in his chapter against the Antidicomarians (those heretics who denied Mary's perpetual virginity).

> The holy virgin may have died and been buried: her falling asleep was with honor, her death in purity, her crown in virginity.
> Or she may have been put to death, as the Scripture says, 'And a sword shall pierce through her soul:' her fame is among the martyrs, and her holy body, by which light rose in the world, rests amid blessings.
> Or she may have remained alive, for God is not incapable of doing whatever he wills. No one knows her end.

St Epiphanius here presents three possibilities. First, Mary could have died and gone to glory. He does not seem to contemplate her being taken up bodily in this case. Second, she could have been martyred. In this case he does not state clearly that she has been taken bodily to heaven. The third possibility he mentions is that she could have been taken body and soul from this world to the glory of heaven without dying.

The saint stops short of declaring that this third is his favored option. He concludes simply by declaring that we don't know her end. He was well aware that the Church had not by then defined the Assumption as a truth of the faith. He was well aware too of the risks of declaring Mary 'immortal' as though she were to be placed alongside the pagan goddesses of Rome.

Still, he puts the bodily Assumption of Mary while she was still alive as the third of his possibilities.

It is customary, in arranging options into three, to place the preferred option last. St Paul said of the Cross of Christ that it is, '... to the Jews a stumbling block, to the Greeks folly, but to those who are called ... the power and the wisdom of God' (1 Corinthians 1:23,24). Clearly St Paul is putting his preferred option last of the three, and I think it is normal to do this.

One doesn't want to play the point for more than it is worth. St Epiphanius states that we just don't know how she finished her earthly life, but it looks likely that he is placing his preferred option at the end, his preferred option being that Mary was taken up to glory bodily, without dying.

Elsewhere in the same chapter he suggests, again without declaring it, that Mary's escape from the dragon in Revelation 12:6,13-17 could be interpreted to mean that she did not die. He mentions this possibility in passing, without developing the idea:

> The Sacred Scriptures do not say that Mary remained in the house of St John, and the probable reason for the silence of Holy Writ concerning Mary's later life may be found in the fact that her life was so completely heavenly and wonderful that mankind could not possibly have borne the spectacle. Perhaps the Apocalypse (12,13) would show by the woman who was snatched from the dragon that Mary escaped death. If she did die, her death was kept hidden, that people might not think too carnally about Mary.

Even as he mentions the possibility that she did not die, he feels the need to mention the contrary possibility, that she did die. And even at that, his instinct is still to suggest that any talk about Mary's death is undesirable, even if it happened, because it would cause people to think 'too carnally' about her.

One can see St Epiphanius the warrior against heresy navigating difficult waters, his instinct to affirm that Mary was taken up without dying, but his unwillingness to declare it as truth for fear of falling into error. He is, to my knowledge, the only major writer in history who suggested that Revelation 12 might indicate that Mary was protected from the dragon's determination to bring about her death. The desire to affirm Mary's freedom from death seems to have entered deep into St Epiphanius's soul.

His preference is even clearer in a passage in the following chapter of the second volume of his book, against the Collyridians, the sect of women priests who offered sacrifices to Mary as if she were a goddess. He again stops short of declaring her bodily Assumption. He still avoids being dogmatic on a question which had not been defined. But he expresses an ardent wish that he could declare the bodily Assumption of Mary while she was still alive.

> 'She has been held in honor for her character and understanding. And if I should say anything more in her praise, she is like Elijah, who was a virgin from his mother's womb, always remained so, and was taken up and has not seen death. ... But Elijah is not to be worshiped even though he is still alive.'

We can see his cautiousness here too. Even when he mentions the assumption of Elijah, which is a biblical truth, he immediately clarifies that Elijah's immortality does not mean he is to be worshiped.

He shows similar caution with regard to Mary. He is not prepared to declare that she was assumed while she was alive; he only compares her to Elijah without stating that she was assumed as he was; but he wishes he could.

St Epiphanius's wish to declare the bodily Assumption of Mary while she was still alive is not a proof that it happened. And yet, that a man of his holiness and integrity should have conceived such a wish is a strong point in favor of the idea.

It is highly significant that the earliest senior churchman to raise the subject of Mary's Assumption also raised the possibility that she was assumed without dying.

No writer before him had expressed any doubt that Mary died. No writer even mentioned the possibility that she mightn't have died. They didn't investigate the matter. Neither the absence of any relics nor the total silence about her place of burial prompted any of them to question whether she died. They didn't try to prove that she died. They took it for granted that she did die. St Epiphanius was the first of the Fathers to raise the possibility that she didn't.

St Epiphanius had a rare gift and a calling from God to fight against heresy. His instincts in the matter of Mary's Assumption have to be taken seriously at the very least, not only because he is recognized as a Father of the Church, but because they show that he was quite a few centuries ahead of his time. Not until around the year 1500 A.D. can we find evidence of anyone even thinking that Mary never died, which is eleven centuries after the lifetime of St Epiphanius.

Yet as early as the 370s St Epiphanius was repeatedly expressing his intuition, and expressing his ardent wish to affirm, that Mary was assumed into heaven while still alive, without ever having died. He couldn't declare it as doctrine at that stage in church history. He could only declare a wish that he could declare it with certainty.

His prophetic instinct cannot be ignored. That he should have conceived a desire to praise God's greatest creature to the ultimate extent; that he should have difficulty constraining himself by giving Mary less praise than Elijah; that he should question any attempt to place limits on his wish to praise her – this in itself is an argument in favor of the view that she was taken up bodily while still alive.

It is not a proof. But when a holy man living under the influence of the Holy Spirit is filled with a desire to praise Mary more rather than less, it is right at least to consider the possibility that such a desire is a holy and a praiseworthy desire, that it comes from the same Holy Spirit, and that it is founded on truth.

St Epiphanius presents a conundrum. 'If I should,' he says; if it were permissible; if the Church should ever define it as dogma … 'If I should say anything more in her praise …' He wants to say more in her praise than he felt at that time permitted to say. '… she is like Elijah, who … was taken up and has not seen death.'

St Epiphanius was not challenging the limits which Church teaching at that time placed on him. He expresses a desire. He suggests the question: Why should I attribute a privilege to Elijah which I must deny to Mary?

We will return to this question later.

500-1000 A.D.

St John Damascene (died 749 A.D.) recorded that at the Council of Chalcedon in 451, the Emperor and Empress Marcion and Pulcheria expressed a wish to take custody of the body of Mary. They were told by St Juvenal, Bishop of Jerusalem, that Mary died in the presence of the apostles but that her tomb, when opened at the request of St Thomas, was found to be empty. The apostles concluded that she had been taken up to heaven bodily.

From this we can see that by the mid-400s there were churchmen, probably a small minority, who had accepted that Mary had been taken up to heaven shortly after her death. St Juvenal presented it as historical fact to the Emperor and Empress. Neither he nor any other churchman, however, had committed the belief to writing. That didn't happen until about three centuries later.

St John Damascene was the first major churchman to advocate the doctrine of the Assumption in writing and under his own name. During his lifetime the teaching was also promoted in the wider church by St Gregory of Tours and St Modestus of Jerusalem.

Near the end of the 500s, at a shrine near Jerusalem, a feast was being celebrated on August 15 each year called the

'Dormition of Our Lady.' It had begun in the mid 400s as the 'Commemoration of the Mother of God.'

In the late 700s, Pope Sergius introduced this Feast in Rome. From there it spread quickly throughout western Europe.

Pope Adrian 1 (772-795 A.D.) changed the name of the Feast from the Dormition of Mary to the Assumption of Mary. This was a very significant shift in emphasis toward the key point of the doctrine, which is that Mary was taken up to heaven bodily by her Son.

The Feast of the Assumption was made an official part of the Divine Office by Pope Leo IV (847-855). From that time, the Assumption was recognized by many as true teaching, though it was not yet defined as dogma.

Before about 1000 A.D. the practices of devotion to Mary varied from individual to individual. Statues of Mary were not placed in churches and there were no widely recognized forms of devotion to Mary. These had to wait until the beginning of the second millennium.

1000-1850 A.D.

From around the year 1000 A.D. statues of Our Lady began appearing in and outside churches, and common devotions to Mary began to gain popularity.

By 1100, beads for the repeated recitation of the Our Father and Hail Mary were used among Christians in some parts of the church. The prayers were not arranged into mysteries until later. In the course of the 1100s the Ave Maria, or Hail Mary, became universal in the church in Europe.

Belief in the Assumption was nearly universal since it had been officially included in the Divine Office in the 800s, but it was still treated as an open theological issue. Christians could believe or not believe in the Assumption without thereby being treated as heretics. Pope Innocent IV (1243-1254 A.D.) treated the Assumption as an opinion that Christians were free to hold or not to hold, as the Church had yet to decide on it.

The great scholastic thinkers of the 1200s, including St Bonaventure and St Thomas Aquinas taught that Mary was not conceived immaculate.

St Bonaventure argued from the death of Mary, which he presumed to be a fact, that Mary could not have been conceived immaculate because if she was then her death would have been an injustice on God's part, and that could not be admitted.

St Bonaventure's position merits close attention. His argument carries the implication that if Mary was conceived immaculate then she couldn't have died, because her death would then have been an injustice on God's part. He was pointing to the logical connection between Mary's Immaculate Conception and her Assumption without death.

He was drawing the connection negatively, on the understanding that she did die, but he was drawing it nonetheless. When the Immaculate Conception was defined as dogma six centuries after his lifetime, then in St Bonaventure's scheme of thinking the conclusion should have been drawn (and was drawn by quite a few), that Mary was assumed without dying.

St Thomas was unable to accept that Mary was conceived without contracting any trace of original sin. He argued that if the Immaculate Conception happened, it would mean that Mary did not need a Savior, and this would be a contradiction of Luke 1:47 in which she declares that her spirit rejoices "in God my Savior."

The Scottish theologian Duns Scotus (1266-1308) resolved the difficulty raised by St Thomas: How could Mary have been conceived immaculate, and still declare that God is her Savior? If she did not contract original sin, how could she have needed a Savior?

Duns Scotus's answer was that the Blood of Christ took advance effect in Mary's case. She was wholly redeemed in advance by the Sacrifice of her Son from the first moment of her conception.

In fact the Blood of Christ had advance effect throughout the history of Israel from the call of Abraham sometime around 1750 B.C. Abraham was called to be the father of the people into whom the Son of God would be born as Messiah and Savior of the world. The Sacrifice on Calvary was what drew God's advance favor on the people of Israel.

Mary's case was the highest and purest point of the case of all of the Israelites who remained faithful and who received the blessings of God in anticipation of the sacrifice of Christ on Calvary. The difference in Mary's case is that she was wholly redeemed by the Blood of Jesus from her first beginning, from her conception, which was immaculate.

Duns Scotus's theological breakthrough opened the way for the confident and certain belief in Mary's Immaculate Conception. Duns Scotus's teaching was adopted by Pope Pius IX in his definition of the dogma of the Immaculate Conception in 1854.

As the doctrine of the Assumption is so closely linked to that of the Immaculate Conception, Duns Scotus's insight opened the way to certainty about the Assumption too.

The centuries from the 1100s to the 1400s saw a gradual succession of changes in the Mass for the Feast of the Assumption by which the resurrection and Assumption of Mary was emphasized more, and her death emphasized less.

The gradual shift of emphasis from Dormition to Assumption led to an understanding among lay Christians in the western church that Mary was assumed into heaven without dying. How widespread had this understanding become? If the works of great artists are the guide, it had become very widespread indeed. It is clear from the work of Titian that by medieval times, in the popular imagination in Europe, Mary was assumed while still alive.

Titian painted his Assumption around 1517 A.D. It shows Mary suddenly being taken up in the midst of ordinary activities among a group of Christians. Clearly therefore, among lay Christians it had become common by about the year 1500 to believe that she was taken up without dying. It must have been fairly common among churchmen too, given that they were the ones who commissioned the paintings of the Assumption.

In general, however, churchmen were more reluctant to declare openly that Mary was assumed without dying. St Alphonsus (1696-1787 A.D.) is a late example of a great saint who was in no doubt that Mary died. It is unusual to find a western saint later than St Bernard affirming her death as fervently as he did.

St Alphonsus spoke of Mary's death in terms of the highest praise, describing it in considerable detail and setting out the effects it had on those present on earth, and on the hosts of heaven as well.

Here is how he expressed his thinking about her death (in Discourse VII, Part 2 of *The Glories of Mary,* taken from the archive.org):

> Death being the punishment of sin, it would seem that the divine mother, all holy and exempt from every stain, should not be subject to death, nor suffer the same misfortune as the children of Adam, who are infected by the poison of sin. But God, wishing Mary in all things to be like Jesus, required, as the Son had died, that the mother should also die.

This is a succinct expression of a tradition about Mary's death that had developed much earlier.

He begins by acknowledging that our first instinct is to declare that the sinless Virgin was not subject to death and that she did not in fact die. He goes on to express the tradition, and he does so wholeheartedly and without any hint of doubt, that God willed her to die in imitation of her Son and as an example holding out the hope of a happy death for all of us.

St Alphonsus was not infallible and his view on the issue is not determinative. The Church has continued to leave us free to believe that Mary was taken up without first dying. Still, St Alphonsus was among the most powerful advocates for the praises of Mary in history. That he adhered to the Dormition tradition is a strong argument in its favor.

But if belief in Mary's Assumption while still alive had become more popular among lay Christians than among churchmen, it had already gained some currency among churchmen too. To my knowledge, St Louis Marie de Montfort, who was still alive when St Alphonsus was growing up, did not state anywhere that Mary died. He didn't deny that she died, but he didn't affirm it either.

I think it is fair to say that by the 1700s it had become normal in western church circles either to remain silent about Mary's death, or to affirm or deny it without showing excessive enthusiasm, out of respect for those who held the opposite view. Those churchmen who believed she didn't die might not have felt free to speak too openly about it, as the issue had not been decided authoritatively in Church doctrine.

But the cat had long been let out of the bag, so to speak. Sometimes a picture speaks more eloquently than words, and that painting by Titian shows us how matters have stood in the popular imagination since about 1500, and probably well before then. The belief that Mary was taken up while still alive had become widespread among lay Christians by the early 1500s.

AFTER 1854

The definition of the Immaculate Conception in 1854 altered the terms of the discourse on Mary. Up to that point is was an open theological question whether she had been immaculately conceived, and the question whether she died did not receive much attention among churchmen.

Before the definition of the Immaculate Conception churchmen did not feel authorized to declare that she did not die. There was too much authority behind the belief that she did die, and the doubt about her Immaculate Conception made the question controversial.

When Mary appeared to the children at Lourdes in 1858, she introduced herself by saying, "I am the Immaculate Conception." In doing so she made known her pleasure at the definition as well as her complete acceptance of the Church's authority to teach the truth in her regard.

By identifying herself with the defined truth of her Immaculate Conception, she also made it known that she regards it as integral to all the truths concerning her. If one were to deny her Immaculate Conception one would not truly know who she is.

After 1854 it was acceptable and even normal for theologians to seriously raise the question whether Mary died, or whether she was assumed while still alive. Indeed, after 1854 it became one of the most widely investigated questions among theologians writing about Mary. Dominic Arnaldi of Genoa, who died in 1895, argued that her complete freedom from sin requires us to believe that she was also free from any subjection to death. One can infer from the writings of St Bonaventure that, if he had lived to see the definition of the Immaculate Conception, he would have been in full agreement with Arnaldi.

In the 1900s the question was taken up by such theologians as Gabriel Roschini and Tibor Gallus S.J.

I am not qualified to offer a technical account of the work of any of these theologians. I only mention them to illustrate that it is now, following the definition of the Immaculate Conception by Pope Pius IX in 1854, normal and acceptable to question whether Mary died and to believe that she didn't. The instinct among lay Christians to affirm her Assumption while still alive can now be shared by churchmen without any fear of censure.

THE ROSARY

Pope Pius XII remarked in *Munificentissimus Deus*, in which he defined the Assumption as a doctrine of the faith, that a mystery of the Rosary is dedicated to the Assumption. In saying this, his intention was to point out that the doctrine he was defining was not something new in the Church's understanding. It was something very ancient.

Mary is involved in each of the original fifteen mysteries of the Rosary. All of the five Joyful Mysteries celebrate the events around Jesus' birth and his earliest years. Mary is directly involved in each of them. She is present at the sorrowful moments of his suffering and death. And she is deeply engaged in the Glorious Mysteries of his Resurrection, his Ascension, and the Descent of the Holy Spirit at Pentecost.

The remaining two Glorious Mysteries concern Mary herself. They are her Assumption into heaven and her Coronation in heaven.

Although it doesn't prove our point, it might be worth noticing that the mysteries of the Rosary contain no reference to Mary's death. Of course this may be simply because her death was of lesser importance and it would not be appropriate to dedicate a whole mystery to it.

On the other hand, if she did die, her death could not be brushed aside as of no importance. Certainly the death of Jesus was the source and origin of our salvation, and it is completely appropriate that an entire five mysteries are dedicated to it. The Rosary is primarily a meditation on the great events of Jesus' life which are the great events of our salvation.

We noted earlier that Mary's participation in these salvific events was not by a death of her own but by her total immersion in the death of her Son as a death suffered also by her in intimate union with him.

That there is no reference to Mary's death in the Rosary is, in my understanding, an indication of this, that she herself didn't die, but took part in our Redemption only by entering totally into the death of her Son.

It is not a proof. It is an indication.

It is one more example of Mary's habit, in her communications with the church, of referring freely to her Assumption but never referring to her death.

There is a tradition that Mary appeared to St Dominic in the year 1214 A.D. and gave him the details of the Rosary, telling him that this was the prayer she wanted her people to say to bring Jesus' salvation to the world. This tradition has been disputed by some scholars, though it has been upheld by others.

Whatever about the scholarship, it is clear that Mary herself has a great love of the Rosary and she exercises great power over our enemy the devil and his wicked angels wherever the Rosary is prayed. There is no doubt that Mary has nurtured and encouraged the recitation of the Rosary among God's people. No doubt she also had an influential hand in designing it.

That the Rosary contains no mystery making mention of her death can be taken as an expression of her wishes. She is always happy to speak of her Assumption. She never speaks of her death.

What does this tell us? That she did die but never talks about it? That doesn't sound right to me. 'Precious in the eyes of the Lord is the death of his faithful.' The Church recognizes saints by the manner of their deaths, and where there is no knowledge of the manner of their deaths no saints are canonized. There have been saints who lived very holy lives, but if the circumstances of their deaths are unknown they will not be formally canonized by the Church.

If Mary did die, I would expect her to speak about it, at least in some of the private revelations she makes to her people. She doesn't, and there is no hint of her death in the mysteries of the Rosary.

'Precious in the eyes of the Lord is the death of his faithful.' That has to mean that if Mary died, her death would be far more precious than the deaths of the other faithful. Her death would have been more worthy of attention than the deaths of all other saints. That the Bible contains no hint of her death, that it is not included among the mysteries of the Rosary, that Mary herself has maintained a noticeably consistent silence about it, that the Church's records of it are dubious to non-existent ...

All of this does not prove that Mary didn't die, but it points strongly in that direction.

RESURRECTION VERSUS ASSUMPTION?

We've been noting the gradual development through the history of the western church from the simple idea of the death of Mary in the first three centuries; to the idea of Dormition, in which the death of Mary is seen as temporary and followed within days by her resurrection and Assumption; to the very gradual rise, through many centuries, in the emphasis and the priority given to her Assumption over her death and resurrection; and finally to a growing sense that she was assumed without dying at all.

I think it is fair to observe that there is something out of proportion in the idea that Mary died, was resurrected, and was assumed into heaven, but that only the Assumption is worthy of attention and veneration.

It Mary followed Jesus in dying and being raised from the dead, then these events call for recognition in the Church's teaching and for veneration in practice.

In the case of Jesus, his death and Resurrection are at the very core of our faith. If he didn't die, we would not be saved from our sins. And if he didn't rise again, our faith would be in vain, as St Paul affirmed (1 Corinthians 15:17).

The Ascension of Jesus is also an article of our faith, but it does not have the central position which our creed accords to his death and to his Resurrection. Scripture describes the Ascension in Acts 1, but nowhere does Scripture teach that if Jesus didn't ascend into heaven we would not be saved from our sins or our faith would be in vain.

In Mary's case, the entire emphasis is on her Assumption, and her death and resurrection are tagged on, if they happened at all. The Assumption is a defined dogma of the faith. We are free to believe in her death and resurrection, and we are free to believe that they didn't happen.

Is this the same as saying that the idea of her death and resurrection is redundant?

If Mary died and was resurrected, I would think her resurrection would be at least as important an event as her Assumption. That her resurrection is treated by the Church as a possibility only, an idea that can be accepted or rejected at the discretion of the individual believer, makes it difficult to take the idea seriously at all.

This brings me back to the first time the idea of Mary's death was brought to my attention. My friends had clearly only just discovered that there is a tradition about the death of Mary, and that this tradition is accepted by many highly creditable churchmen, and they found the idea as mystifying as I did. They asked for my opinion. My first instinct was to respond that if Mary died we would have to talk about her resurrection first and foremost. Her Assumption would come second.

I don't claim that my first instincts set the rule of faith. And yet I have never heard that first objection answered. If Mary died and rose again before being assumed into heaven, why do we brush aside her death and resurrection and consider only her Assumption? Why is her resurrection totally absent from Scripture, and from the Divine Office, and from the Rosary? Why, if her resurrection happened, are we under no obligation to believe in it, or to venerate it, or to give it any mention in our prayers?

The most convincing explanation I can think of for all of this is that her resurrection didn't happen because she didn't die. The problems with the idea of Mary's death and resurrection are resolved very easily if we understand that she was assumed into heaven without dying.

ENOCH, MOSES

The Bible tells of two men who were taken up to heaven without dying, and of a third man who was very likely taken up shortly after his death. The two who were taken up without dying are Enoch and Elijah. The one who was probably taken up after his death is Moses. We will now take a look at the biblical evidence for the assumptions of Enoch and Moses before turning to the much more detailed biblical record of the assumption of Elijah.

Enoch
Genesis provides scant detail on Enoch's assumption.

> In all, Enoch lived for three hundred and sixty five years. Enoch walked with God, then he was no more, because God took him.   - Genesis 5:23,24

The text does not say that he lived for so many years and then he died, as is normal in such records. It says that he lived so long walking with God and then God took him. In case there might be any doubt about what this means, it is elaborated in the New Testament, where Enoch's assumption is plainly stated: he was taken up without experiencing death.

By faith Enoch was taken up and did not taste death. He was no more, because God took him; because before his assumption he had this testimony, that he pleased God. Now it is impossible to please God without faith.

- Hebrews 11:5,6

Moses

The Old Testament record of the death of Moses suggests that he was taken up after his death but does not affirm it beyond doubt. At the end of his life, after Moses had led the Israelites out of Egypt and through forty years wandering in the wilderness, and on to the conquest of the land east of the Jordan, the Lord spoke to him. He reminded him that he had not been wholly innocent in the matter of the Israelite's rebellion at Meribah in the desert, and that he was therefore not going to cross the Jordan with his people and take part in the conquest of the land west of the Jordan. He was to climb Mount Nebo alone and end his earthly life there.

Moses had climbed the mountain of Horeb alone to receive the words of the Law on the tablets of stone. None of the other Israelites were to join him as he ascended Horeb. There he spoke to Yahweh face to face with no other human being present.

Now, at the end of his life, he was to climb Mount Nebo, again on his own, to meet Yahweh there and to die there with no other human being present.

> Then, leaving the Plains of Moab, Moses went up Mount Nebo, the peak of Pisgah opposite Jericho, and Yahweh showed him the whole country ... There in the land of Moab, Moses, servant of Yahweh, died as Yahweh decreed; he buried him in the valley, in the land of Moab, opposite Beth-Peor; but to this day no one has ever found his grave. - Deuteronomy 34:1-6

There is no question that Moses died. The text states it clearly. It is also clear that he died there at the top of the mountain. The Lord had already decreed it.

> "Die on the mountain you have climbed, and be gathered to your people." - Deuteronomy 32:50

His burial, however, was in the valley, in the land of Moab. And the one who buried him was 'he,' Yahweh.

The account thus ends in deliberate mystery. The burial of Moses may have been attended by other Israelites, because they wept for him for thirty days there on the Plains of Moab

(Deuterunomy 34:8), but this is not at all certain, as the text states that 'he,' Yahweh, buried him and that from that day to this no one has ever known where his grave is.

Though it does not state it explicitly, the text supports the tradition that Moses was raised by God again before his flesh corrupted, and was taken up bodily into heaven.

The reference in Jude v.9 to a dispute between Michael the Archangel and Satan about the body of Moses is sometimes taken as confirmation that Moses was assumed after his death, as the apostle was referring to an apocryphal work called *The Assumption of Moses.*

I don't believe Jude is confirming that Moses was assumed in that verse. For one thing, *The Assumption of Moses* seems to be a misnomer as it doesn't actually claim that Moses was assumed. For another, Jude's point in this verse is to warn Christians against engaging in angry conversation with demons; he is not issuing any kind of adjudication on the question whether Moses was assumed; the verse doesn't refer to this issue at all.

The assumption of Moses is not openly declared, either in the Old Testament or in the New, but it finds strong confirmation in Luke's account of the Transfiguration of Jesus:

> And it happened that, as he was praying, the aspect of his countenance was altered, and his clothing became white and glistening. And suddenly there were two men talking to him; they were Moses and Elijah appearing in glory, and they spoke of his death which he would accomplish in Jerusalem.   - Luke 9:29-31

Moses and Elijah appeared in glory together on Mount Tabor, speaking with Jesus in the presence of the apostles Peter and James and John.

Elijah had been taken up bodily, we know that. The text doesn't say that Moses had been taken up bodily, but when it describes both Moses and Elijah 'appearing in glory,' this is a very strong indicator that Moses appeared in a glorified body as Elijah did. If Moses had appeared as a disembodied soul, his state of glory would have been so different from Elijah's that it would be anomalous do describe the glory of both in the same words.

I think it reasonable to conclude from this that the body of Moses was not allowed to decay on the plains of Moab. It is reasonable, I believe, to take Luke's description of Moses and Elijah appearing in glory together on Mount Tabor as confirmation that Moses had been taken up bodily shortly after he died.

Moses is praised by God in the Bible as few others are praised. Yet he is criticized by God too.

"Because with the other Israelites you broke faith with me at the Waters of Meribah-Kadesh in the desert of Zin, because you did not make my holiness clear to the Israelites, you may only see the land from the outside; you cannot enter the land which I am giving to the Israelites."
- Deuteronomy 32:51,52

Neither Enoch nor Elijah received any such criticism. They were taken up while still alive. Moses was probably taken up, but it is not plainly stated, and he died first.

Should we take it that the assumption of Moses was a lesser assumption than the assumption of Enoch and the assumption of Elijah?

The point would be a petty one if we were seeking to compare the praiseworthiness of the three and to find Moses inferior in merit to the other two. Certainly it is not for us to judge between the great figures of the Bible.

But if we are looking for biblical hints as to whether Mary, Mother of God, the greatest of all his creatures, was assumed while alive or after she had first died, then our question might be a helpful and even a necessary question to ask.

Why would we want to attribute the inferior form of assumption to the greatest of all God's creatures? Why would we want to accord a lesser assumption to the one in whom God himself was pleased to be imprisoned for the first nine months of his earthly life?

If we have a choice between the two, should we not at least wish to accord Mary the greater rather than the lesser Assumption?

ELIJAH

The description of Elijah's assumption in 2 Kings 2 is by far the most complete description of an assumption in the whole of Scripture. It is so much more detailed, more startlingly vivid, more revealing of what it means to be assumed, than any other references to assumption in the Bible that there is really no comparison between it and them.

The account begins with Elijah trying to shake off his companion and disciple Elisha. Elijah, being a great prophet, knew that he was about to be taken from this world. He had business to do with the Lord, and he didn't want anyone trying to hold him back. Elisha, also a great prophet, knew it too, and was determined not to leave him alone.

"You stay here," Elijah said to Elisha as he set off from Gilgal. "The Lord is sending only me to Bethel" (2 Kg 2:2). "As the Lord lives and as you yourself live, I will not leave you," Elisha rejoined. So they set off for Bethel.

The company of prophets at Bethel came out to meet the two of them, and informed Elisha, as if he didn't know, that the Lord would carry Elijah away that day.

Elijah then told Elisha to stay in Bethel, because the Lord had told only him to go to Jericho. Elisha was just as insistent that he would not let Elijah out of his sight.

At Jericho the same thing happened. There too the brotherhood of prophets 'informed' Elisha of what was about to happen to Elijah. Elijah told Elisha to stay at Jericho, "because the Lord is sending only me to the Jordan."

By now fifty prophets accompanied them as they walked toward the river Jordan. The fifty stood at a distance as Elijah and Elisha arrived at the river bank. The waters of the Jordan were parted when Elijah rolled up his cloak and struck the river with it, and the two walked in on dry ground.

Elijah asked Elisha if he had any last request to make. "Give me a double share of your spirit," Elisha requested. Elijah said it was a hard thing to grant, but if Elisha saw him as he was being taken up, it would be granted to him.

> And it came to pass, as they still went on, and talked, that behold, there appeared a chariot of fire, and horses of fire, and parted them both asunder; and Elijah went up by a whirlwind into heaven. And Elisha saw it, and he cried, "My father, my father, the chariot of Israel, and the horsemen thereof!" And he saw him no more.
>
> - 2 Kings 2:11,12

The mantle of Elijah had fallen from him. Elisha took it and struck the waters of the Jordan with it, and they separated.

When he returned to the fifty prophets, they recognized that he had inherited the spirit of Elijah, and they bowed before him.

They then begged Elisha to let them go looking for Elijah, in case the Lord had taken him up only to leave him down again somewhere. Elisha disapproved of their desire to go looking for him. When they pressed him, he reluctantly let them go looking for him and they searched for three days, but had to return and admit failure. "Didn't I tell you not to go," Elisha chided.

From the biblical account of Elijah's assumption we can pick out a number of features:

There is, from the beginning, a prophetic foreknowledge in Elijah and in his fellow prophets of what is about to happen, that he is to be taken up.

There is, among his fellow prophets, a strong resistance to being separated from him. They really don't want him to leave them. Elisha insists on being with him right to the end. The others insist on setting out in search of him even after he has been taken up.

There is the sudden, dramatic appearance of a chariot of fire and horses of fire which 'parted them both asunder.' They were forcibly separated. The gulf between this world and the heavenly world came and hit Elisha in the face so to speak. Elijah was being taken up, and Elisha was to remain below. There was no helping it. The separation was very painful, and very necessary.

"My father, my father, the chariot of Israel and the horsemen thereof!" Elisha cried out in grief at the loss of the one who had spoken the words given by God, the one who had called Israel back from the deadly works of idolatry to the worship of the living God, the one who had brought the power and the relief, the integrity and the truth of the living word of God back among his people.

The suffering of Elisha from the loss of his master Elijah was not ignored by God. The very act of grieving, the very reverence given to the prophet of Yahweh, drew forth the mercy of God, who caused the prophet's spirit to enter into Elisha so that he could carry on the work his master Elijah had begun.

At first he didn't realize it. Far from feeling any transfer of power to himself, he could only express his feeling of despair. Elijah was taken up in the whirlwind and disappeared. Elisha stooped down and picked up the mantle which Elijah had left behind.

The mantle of Elijah seemed to Elisha to be mocking him. He did what came naturally to him; he did what he had seen Elijah doing: he struck the waters of the Jordan with the mantle, not in hope, but in despair. "Where is the God of Elijah?" he cried in desperation as he struck the waters.

Then the unthinkable happened. What a shock he must have received when the waters of the Jordan parted as soon as he struck them, and he was able to cross on dry ground, just as had happened for Elijah.

By the time he got back to the fifty prophets, they recognized him as the one in whom Elijah's spirit and power endured. Elijah had been taken up, but his work, his spirit, his power, lived on in Israel.

Elijah's departure had looked like the end for Elisha. He had resisted it to the last moment. Now, however, it had suddenly become clear that Elijah's departure was also a beginning. God was building up in Elisha the confidence to carry on the work he had begun in Elijah and to exercise in Israel the great gift he had already manifestly been given, a double share in the spirit of Elijah.

This description from the Second Chapter of the Second Book of Kings, of the assumption of Elijah, gives us a kind of biblical blueprint, telling us what an assumption looks like.

It would be useful to know if there is any other passage in the Bible in which the features of the assumption of Elijah are present, even if they are only hinted at. Can we find such a passage?

I believe we can. I've written about this elsewhere and will be as brief as possible here. The passage in which at least some of the features of the events in 2 Kings 2 are hinted at can be found in the Song of Songs. We will take a look at this Book in the next chapter.

THE SHULAMITE IN THE SONG OF SONGS

The Song of Songs is written in the language of original innocence, when Adam and Eve 'were naked and were not ashamed' (Genesis 2:25). It consists of dialogue between the Bride and the Groom, with a few passages interposed in the voice of the author.

It is a song of praise answering praise answering praise. One of the first questions we ask in reading this Book of the Bible is, Who is praising whom? If we can answer that question we have the key to understanding the whole work.

It has variously been read as a dialogue between the bride and groom in a human marriage; between Yahweh and his people Israel; between Christ and his church.

We can read it in each of these ways, and we can see references to all of them in the text. There is nothing wrong with this. We often find multiple layers of meaning in the language used in the Bible. It is right to read the Song of Songs, at least in part, as a dialogue between the groom and the bride in a human marriage, and between Yahweh and his people Israel, and between Christ and his church.

There are references to each of these in the Song of Songs. However, if you restrict yourself to any one of these levels of meaning you will gain only limited understanding of the text. Some passages will remain baffling to you.

If you only see the Song of Songs as God's eulogy of human marriage, for example, you will quickly run into trouble. The setting in much of the Song of Songs is the household of King Solomon and his growing harem. The bride is his new and favorite addition to the harem.

The problem with seeing the Song of Songs as God's eulogy of human marriage is that it would imply that God's model marriage is located in the burgeoning harem of King Solomon, which eventually numbered no fewer than 1,000 locked up women, comprising 700 royal 'wives' and 300 'concubines' (1 Kings 11:3).

Solomon allowed the foreign women to bring their idols into his household and to make sacrifices to them. In old age he even became a follower of false gods himself. It became his downfall, the reason his name cannot be mentioned with unambiguous honor, and the reason his kingdom split in two immediately after his death, as the Lord prophesied to him in 1 Kings 11:11-13.

The idea that King Solomon and his thousand member harem is to be understood as God's ideal conjugal arrangement can be dismissed without too much delay. We need to dig deeper to arrive at a satisfying understanding of what God is saying to us in the Song of Songs. We will get much further with it if we see it as a dialogue between God and his people Israel, or Christ and his church.

Either of these readings, however, if we restrict ourselves to them, will still leave us with passages which we find incomprehensible.

The key is to see Mary prophetically written into every line in the Song of Songs. Israel and the church follow in her footsteps, but Mary, the greatest flower of Israel and the Queen and Mother of the church, is the first point of reference on the Bride's side of the conversation. Once we begin to read it this way the mist begins to lift and we can arrive at a satisfying, even a delightful understanding of what God is saying in all parts of the text.

St Bernard began his great Commentary on the Song of Songs by observing that, like all of the Old Testament, it is concerned first and above all with the Incarnation of Christ. The whole of the Old Testament is God's account of how and why he created the entire material universe.

He created it for Christ. It was in the mind of the God of Love from the beginning that God would take a body, because in this way and in no other could he give himself to his creature not restricted by the creature's limited capacity to receive him, but in all the fullness of his own Godhead.

He could not do this spiritually. A pure spirit cannot receive God in all the fullness of his Godhead. An embodied spirit can, because in Christ God has himself become an embodied spirit, able to give himself to other embodied spirits in all the fullness of God's own Godhead.

The Incarnation, the Eucharist, is the reason for the creation of the material universe.

That is why the coming of Christ is at the center of the Bible. Everything in the Old Testament leads up to the coming of Christ. Everything in the New Testament describes it and leads from it.

It is not surprising therefore to find that the Song of Songs is concerned above all with the Incarnation of Christ.

God needed a people to be born into. He began forming this people when he called Abraham, about seventeen and a half centuries before the Incarnation of Christ.

> For verily he took not on him the nature of angels, but he took on him the seed of Abraham.   - Hebrews 2:16

The history of God's family Israel led up, over those seventeen and a half centuries, to the woman prophesied in Genesis 3:15. She would be formed as the Mother of God by living among the Temple virgins in Jerusalem. She would be formed, as her people were formed, in the crucible of affliction. Her life would be a succession of troubles intermixed with moments of joy beyond what can be described. She would be wholly free of the stain of any sin from the first moment of her conception. She would be the creature through whom the Son of God could worthily be born into our world.

Mary is at the very centre of salvation history.

That is why it is no surprise to find Mary at the centre of the Song of Songs. She is at the centre of God's plan to take a body. The love song which is the Song of Songs is a dialogue of praise between God and Mary, with the church following, and it concerns the Incarnation of Christ as St Bernard made clear at the beginning of his Commentary.

The praises of God for Mary become particularly intense from 6:4 onward. In the preceding long passage, from 5:1 to 6:3, the Passion, death and Resurrection of Our Lord have been symbolically described.

Mary has accompanied him through the streets of Jerusalem. She has been with him through the terrible moments, up to the moment he breathed his last on Calvary. She has confronted the unbelief of the apostles and other disciples with a song of praise for her Son that could only have been inspired from heaven, in which she compares him in all particulars with the Temple in Jerusalem, reviving their hope and their faith and, on the first Easter Sunday morning, sending them to the tomb to look for him and to learn the truth, that he is not dead, he is risen.

From that point on, God's praises of Mary ascend to heights that no human imagination could ever have invented.

> "You are fair as Tirzah, my beloved,
> enchanting as Jerusalem,
> terrible as an army with banners.
> Turn your eyes away from me,
> for they have overcome me!"
> - Song of Songs 6:4,5

God is now praising Mary so highly that he even seems to be a little scared of her! 'Turn your eyes away from me, for they have overcome me!' This is a prophetic reference to the authority Mary is given over God himself when she becomes his Mother.

Such authority could never be exercised by any creature who was not herself wholly submitted to God; her authority is nevertheless real; Jesus will not refuse anything his mother asks for; he will treat her requests as commands; he does this knowing, of course, that Mary's requests will always be entirely in line with the promptings of the Holy Spirit and the will of the Father.

The praises of God for the creature who glorifies him most continue. He goes on to raise Mary to her position as Queen of queens and Mother of the church:

> "There are sixty queens and eighty concubines
> and virgins without number
> but my dove, my undefiled is only one;
> she is the only one of her mother,
> the choice one of her that bore her.
> The daughters saw her and declared her blessed,
> the queens and concubines have sung her praises:
> 'Who is she that arises like the dawn,
> fair as the moon, clear as the sun,
> and terrible as an army with banners.'"
>
> - Song of Songs 6:8-10

There is a hint of her Assumption in these words, 'arises like the dawn.' She is raised up and filled with a wholly new power, the power of heaven making her fair as the moon, clear as the sun, and terrible against all the armies of hell. Mary's Assumption into the heavenly realms freed her of all restrictions in acting as the Queen and leader of God's armies.

But though there is a hint of her Assumption in these words, this is not the text of the Song of Songs that reminds us of the assumption of Elijah. That text is the one immediately following, in verses 6:11-7:1.

Mary goes 'down to the nut orchard to see the fresh shoots of the valley, to see if the vines are budding and the pomegranates are in flower.' Mary is always the gardener. She is always looking for the new growth, the fruits of the works of God among his people.

Then, in the midst of her 'gardening' activity, something happens that takes her completely by surprise:

> "Before ever I knew, my desire had thrown me
> onto the chariots of Amminadib.
> 'Return, return O Shulamite!
> Return, return, that we may look upon you!'
> 'Why do you look at the Shulamite,
> she dances between two armies?'"
>
> - Song of Songs 6:11-7:1

At first sight, the setting of this beautiful passage is a playful part of wedding celebrations in the ancient Middle East. A game is played (we can surmise that one name of the game may have been The Chariots of Amminadib, as suggested in the text).

The family of the groom line up on one side. The family of the bride line up on the other. The bride herself dances down the middle between the two lines, with the groom waiting at the end to take her and dance away with her. While she is progressing down the middle, she turns now toward one family, now toward the other, as the families take their turns raucously calling on her to turn toward them while she is turned toward the family of the other.

The groom, affecting jealousy, or perhaps actually feeling it, chides the families in a reminder that a new family has been formed now and she belongs to the new family, not to either of the old ones.

This game, played at weddings, gives us the key to what scholars call the 'literal' meaning of the text, the meaning in the mind of the human author when he wrote it. It strikes me as a delightful game with deep symbolic significance, but here in the Song of Songs it has prophetic reference to Mary, and the marriage being celebrated is not a human marriage.

It is very important, when seeking the meaning of a prophetic scriptural text, to understand that the meaning intended by the Holy Spirit goes far beyond the 'literal' meaning, the meaning intended by the human author. The entire Old Testament explodes with new meaning in the light of the New Testament, and although the human authors of the Old Testament texts may have had an inkling about their references to the coming of the Messiah, their understanding of the prophetic significance of what they were writing was limited and greatly inferior to the understanding of the Holy Spirit who inspired them to write it.

Prophecy in the Bible is not a product of human invention. It is a product of the action of the Holy Spirit. Scripture itself sets out this principle:

> We must recognize that the interpretation of scriptural prophecy is not a matter for individual interpretation. For no prophecy ever came from the will of men, but holy men spoke for God as they were moved by the Holy Spirit.   - 2 Peter 1:20,21

The Old Testament is filled with examples of events whose significance only became clear in the New Testament, with the coming of the Messiah. Jacob's dream of a ladder for example, on which the angels of God were ascending and descending (Genesis 28:12) remained a mystery until Jesus explained what it meant:

"In all truth I tell you, you will see heaven open and the angels of God ascending and descending upon the Son of Man. - John 1:51

This is why it is right to seek the meaning of Old Testament texts in the light of the New Testament. We have no need to be satisfied with the 'literal' interpretation, because the intention of the human author does not exhaust the richness of meaning intended by the Holy Spirit. If we are having difficulty with a text, we need to keep Church teaching in mind, to avoid straying outside it, and we need to pray to the Holy Spirit for the gift of understanding. He will certainly help us.

When Mary was taken up, she entered the heavenly realms, but she did not lose sight of the church on earth. Because she never died, she never wholly left the earth. As Mother of the Church, she is intimately engaged with all of us, deeply concerned with our salvation, eager to tend the garden of the church and to see the fruits come forth, filled with the power of her heavenly body to fulfill all her responsibility for each of us down to an unimaginable degree of detail.

She dances between two armies, the Church Triumphant in heaven, and the Church Militant on earth. She does not forget us. She is concerned with each of our struggles and she helps all those who ask for her help here on earth, even as she enjoys the very life of God with the saints in glory.

We are now ready to compare this passage from the Song of Songs with the much more detailed description of the assumption of Elijah, the only detailed description of an assumption in Scripture. We begin with the common features of the two descriptions, the account of the assumption of Elijah in 2 Kings 2, which we looked at in the previous chapter, and the much briefer account of the Assumption of Mary in the Song of Songs 6:11-7:1.

In both descriptions:

The scene begins in the presence of a group of fellow believers, kindred spirits. In Elijah's case it is Elisha and the community of fifty prophets. In Mary's case it is the 'fresh shoots of the valley,' a group of newly converted Christians in the very early church.

There is a sudden appearance of a chariot or chariots.

There is a sudden separation.

Those left behind in the separation protest and are unwilling to be separated.

A senior voice chides them for their protests and encourages them to accept the separation.

The same senior voice assures them that though the person assumed has left them, something of their spirit has remained behind.

This is an impressive set of similarities in a description as short as the one we are considering from the Song of Songs. On adverting to the similarities it becomes difficult to avoid seeing at the very least a possibility that these two descriptions in Scripture refer to similar events.

There are a number of differences too:

Elijah's assumption is expected, both by Elijah himself and by Elisha and the other prophets. Mary, by contrast, is taken completely by surprise, 'before ever she was aware,' and those present are thrown into sudden consternation too.

(It is possible that this contrast might not be as sharp as it looks. Mary may have had a prophetic intuition of her Assumption, and Elijah might have had no prior knowledge of the manner of his assumption; the appearance of the fiery chariot might have taken him as much by surprise as Mary – but we are not told.)

Mary is not taken up in a whirlwind as Elijah was. The 'protesters' in both cases are given assurance in connection with the separation, but they are assured for different reasons:

the fifty prophets see that Elisha has inherited the mantle and the spirit of Elijah; Elijah is definitely gone and is not coming back, but his work in Israel continues powerfully in Elisha.

In the case of Mary's Assumption, there is no one to take her place when she goes; the 'protesters' are assured rather that she is not being taken away from them at all. Her Assumption does not mean that she is leaving one army to join another; it means that she is 'dancing between two armies.' She is still with us, not only in spirit, but in flesh and blood and with a Heart that still beats with love for us.

We have lost nothing by her Assumption. No, her Assumption has set her free to be with all of us, all the vast hordes of the church through history, with none of the limitations placed on the earthbound. She has been assumed into heaven even as she remains wholly engaged with us here on earth.

It seems clear that this passage in the Song of Songs 6:11-7:1 contains enough of the features of the description of Elijah's assumption in 2 Kings 2 to qualify as a description of an Assumption too. It is much more allusive, much less detailed, but there are sufficient reminders of Elijah's assumption to indicate that we are looking at a similar event.

Why, if I am right, did the Holy Spirit provide a much more complete description of Elijah's assumption? If he really does intend us to glean the truth about Mary's Assumption from that passage in the Song of Songs, why did he not fill in the details as he did for Elijah?

One could come up with a number of answers to this. For one thing, the language of the Bible is generally patriarchal. Women are seen as ancillary to men in Scripture. During her lifetime Mary did not have a high public profile. The only detailed description of any part of Mary's earthly life is in the Gospel of Luke, who was a Hellenistic Jew and who therefore felt less need to keep a woman's life hidden. And even Luke provided detail on Mary only so far as it was relevant to the beginnings of Jesus' earthly life.

The New Testament proclamation is centered on Jesus, and, for the reasons we've seen earlier, an easily discerned emphasis on Mary's Assumption, either in the New Testament or the Old, might have confused the early Church's attempts to achieve clarity on the truths concerning Christ. Hence the gradualness of the development of the Church's understanding of the doctrine of the Assumption was not an accident. It was intended by the Holy Spirit. The truths about Mary were not revealed to us all at once.

These are just a few of the reasons it might have been desirable for the truth about Mary's Assumption to be given only veiled reference in Scripture

I am nonetheless strongly of the opinion that the passage we have been looking at in the Song of Songs is a description of Mary's Assumption, more complete, more satisfying, more aligned with the description of the assumption of Elijah, than it appears at first sight.

If I am right, it also amounts to strong evidence that Mary's Assumption was similar to the assumption of Elijah rather than the assumption of Moses. In other words, it amounts to strong evidence that she did not die but was taken up while still alive.

This is consistent also with the degree of praise given to Mary by God in the Song of Songs, which is praise without measure.

It need not surprise us to find an indication of Mary's Assumption in the Song of Songs, because all of the other great Marian dogmas are prophetically indicated in this Book as well.

I believe it makes sense to take a look at the references to the other Marian doctrines in this Book of the Bible, because it they are all there, this adds confirmation to our view that the Assumption is there as well. It would be strange if only the dogma of the Assumption were absent.

We will also consider whether the Dormition is indicated in the Song of Songs. If it is not, but all the other great Marian dogmas are, this would add further confirmation to the view that Mary was assumed without dying.

We will take a look at the references to the other great dogmas in the next chapter.

THE MARIAN DOCTRINES IN THE SONG OF SONGS

The New Testament gives us little information about Our Lady. What information it does give us is condensed and filled with significance; we can extract a world of meaning from it; but apart from the first two chapters of the Gospel of Luke, the details provided are scant.

To fill in the picture we need to turn to the Old Testament, to the Song of Songs. This Book of the Bible fills in much of the detail omitted in the New Testament.

The New Testament is silent about the end of Mary's life on earth. It does not tell us explicitly about her Assumption into heaven. We can infer her Assumption from Revelation 12, but it is not directly stated even there.

We have expressed the view that the passage in Song of Songs 6:11-7:1, because of its common features with the account of Elijah's assumption in 2 Kings 2, is a brief, fleeting description of Mary's Assumption.

It would be intriguing to know if there is also evidence of her death in the Song of Songs. Does this Book of the Bible provide any evidence in favor of the Dormition?

I believe the answer to this question is no. All the other Marian doctrines are mentioned, most of them several times, as we will see in this chapter, but on the Dormition the Song of Songs is, so far as I can find, wholly silent. There is one passage which could be argued about, and we will discuss it in detail in the next chapter, but on close examination I believe it only serves to confirm the conclusion: There is no evidence for the Dormition in the Song of Songs.

We will now look at some of the texts confirming the other great Marian doctrines.

The Immaculate Conception is plainly stated:

> You are all fair, my love;
> there is no spot in you.
> - Song of Songs 4:7

This reads like a dictionary definition of the Immaculate Conception. Further confirmation is given in the following verses:

> As a lily among brambles,
> so is my beloved among maidens.
> - Song of Songs 2:2

> My dove, my undefiled, is only one.
> - Song of Songs 6:9

The perpetual virginity of Mary is clear from these lines:

> A garden enclosed is my sister, my bride,
> a spring closed up, a fountain sealed.
> - Song of Songs 4:12

The Virgin Birth is also clear from this passage combined with the passages about her fruitfulness which follow.

The doctrine of Mary, Mother of God is indirectly affirmed in passages such as this one, which refers to the authority she exercises in her Son's regard:

> Turn your eyes away from me,
> for they have overcome me.
> - Song of Songs 6:5

It is also indicated affectionately in some of her expressions about her infant Son, like this one, after the Magi had visited and brought gifts for the new king including myrrh:

> "A bundle of myrrh is my well beloved to me,
> he shall lie all night between my breasts."
> - Song of Songs 1:13

The Coronation and Queenship of Mary are very clear in the outbreak of praise for her in Chapter 6, where she is placed above all other queens:

> There are sixty queens and eighty concubines
> and virgins without number.
> My dove, my undefiled is only one.
> - Song of Songs 6:8,9

Mary's spousal relationship with the Holy Spirit is stated plainly too, in these lines (which presage the Angel Gabriel's words to Mary in Luke 1:35 – "The Holy Spirit will come upon you, and the power of the Most High will cover you with its shadow; therefore the child which will be born of you will be called the Son of God"):

> I sat down under his shadow with great delight,
> and his fruit was sweet to my taste.
> He has taken me into his cellar,
> and his banner over me is love.
> - Song of Songs 2:3,4

This passage can also, via its link with the 'Son of God' reference in Luke 1:35, be taken as indirect support for the doctrine of Mary Mother of God.

The doctrines which have been generally accepted but which are not a defined part of our faith are also there in the Song of Songs. That Mary is the Co-redemptrix and the Mediatrix of All Graces is clear from this passage, where the 'apple tree,' which is the Cross of Christ on Calvary, is the place where we were all born into the realm of divine grace by our Mother who stood under it:

> I raised you up under the apple tree,
> there where your mother conceived you,
> there where she who conceived you brought you forth.
> - Song of Songs 8:5

This doctrine is also present in the passage in which King Solomon triumphantly rides into Jerusalem on a chariot, having returned from his bride's home in the north. The passage ends with a declaration by a herald, calling on the daughters of Zion to come and see King Solomon wearing the diadem with which his mother crowned him on the day of his wedding. The diadem is explained in other scriptures (see Isaiah 62:3 for example), as God's kingdom, his people who form a 'princely diadem' in the hand of our God.

> Daughters of Zion, come and see king Solomon
> wearing the diadem with which his mother crowned him
> on the day of his wedding,
> on the day of the gladness of his heart.
>
> - Song of Songs 3:11

The princely diadem, which symbolizes Jesus' bride, his kingdom, his church, is the diadem with which his Mother will crown him on the great Day, the Day that will never end.

The princely diadem is explained in one of the locutions in Fr Gobbi's book for the Marian Movement of Priests. The locution is recorded by Fr Gobbi as taking place on the Solemnity of Christ the King, 1986:

> "Today, in the glory of paradise and in the purifying light of purgatory, I am accepting the homage of the whole pilgrim church on earth, in order to offer, together with you all, the crown of his royalty to Jesus Christ, our God, our Savior and our King."
>
> - MMP 339

These words illustrate just how profoundly Mary's conceptions are bound up with the word of God, which she has 'pondered in her heart' from the beginning. She is saying here that the 'diadem' that crowns the kingship of Christ and gladdens his heart is not made of gold or jewelry, however precious. The only diadem he is interested in is the acceptance we his people, 'the vast number which no man could count' (Revelation 7:9), give to him and to his rule over us. Our acceptance of his love and of his authority over us is 'the diadem with which his Mother crowns him on the day of his wedding, on the day of the gladness of his heart.'

So we can see that all the Church's doctrines concerning Mary are prophesied at least once in the Song of Songs. I can't find a single exception. It need come as no surprise to find the Assumption there among them in verses 6:11-7:1.

Is the Dormition prophesied? Is there a reference to Mary's death in the Song of Songs? We will turn to this question in the next chapter.

THE DORMITION IN THE SONG OF SONGS?

Nowhere can I find it convincingly stated or indicated in the Song of Songs that Mary died before she was taken up. The Dormition is, to my knowledge, the only widely accepted doctrine in regard to Mary that is absent from this book of the Bible.

The passage that might be argued about is verse 6:11, which comes immediately before the description of the Assumption in 6:12 and 7:1. If we compare 6:11 with 6:2 we notice a formal similarity between them which we might at first take as indicating a similarity of meaning. We will compare these two verses at some length here in an attempt to ensure that we are treating the issue as objectively and honestly as possible.

In 6:2 Mary speaks of where Jesus has been during the time his body lay dead in the tomb. She is speaking in answer to the question of the disciples, Where is Jesus gone? Their question follows Mary's dialogue with the disciples after Jesus' death, and after she had begun encouraging them to go looking for him at the time of his Resurrection. She had charged them in 5:8, if they found him, to pass on her message that she is sick with love. She needs to see him. They had responded out of the depths of their hopelessness with utter incredulity: Who do you think he is? Haven't you heard? They've done away with him! He's in the tomb! (Verse 5:9)

Mary replied with a song of praise that was wholly miraculous (5:10-16). It was a detailed description of the Temple in Jerusalem, by which she let the disciples know that Jesus, being the very Temple of God, cannot be destroyed.

Their faith and hope were awakened by Mary's majestic song of praise. They had been asking, Who do you think he is? Now there were asking, Where is he gone, that we may seek him too? (6:1)

Mary answered:

> My beloved went down into his garden,
> to the beds of spices,
> to pasture his flock on the grass,
> and to gather lilies.
>
> - Song of Songs 6:2

The gathering of lilies here refers to Jesus, having redeemed them by the Blood of his Cross, descending into the realms of the dead and calling many of them out of their imprisonment and into the glory of Paradise to await the resurrection of their bodies too. It is a reference to the doctrine, included in the Apostles Creed, that during the time his body was in the tomb awaiting Resurrection, Jesus went down among the souls of the dead, announced their liberation to them, and brought them with him to Paradise. This doctrine is also found in the New Testament:

> In the body he was put to death, in the spirit he was raised to life, and in the spirit he went to preach to the spirits in prison.
> - 1 Peter 3:18,19

This teaching is further elaborated by Peter:

> This is why the gospel was brought to the dead as well so that, though in their bodies they had undergone the judgment that faces all humanity, in their spirit they might enjoy the life of God.
> - 1 Peter 4:6

The text of Song of Songs 6:2 is a prophetic reference to these events, which occurred in the hours between Jesus' death on Good Friday afternoon and his Resurrection early on Easter Sunday morning.

Immediately before the description of Mary's Assumption, there is the passage which, at first sight, looks a little like Verse 6:2:

> I went down into the garden of nuts
> to see the fresh fruits of the valley,
> and to see if the vines were budding
> and the pomegranate trees were in flower.
> - Song of Songs 6:11

If one were only looking at the opening phrases of 6:2 and 6:11, it would be possible to see them as mirroring each other, and hence it might be tempting to read 6:11 as an account of Mary descending into Purgatory after her death and before her resurrection and Assumption to review the progress of the souls being purified there. If Jesus went among the dead after his death and before his Resurrection, might Mary have been led on a similar journey? If I were a believer in the Dormition I would want to explore whether the passage can be read in this way.

It could be argued that the opening phrase in each verse, together with the context – 6:2 comes immediately after the dialogue concerning Jesus' death; 6:11 comes immediately before the description of Mary's Assumption – points to a parallel in significance between the two verses, and suggests that 6:11 is an account of Mary's death and descent among the dead in Purgatory.

One major problem with this is that you can only sustain the argument if you ignore the other terms in the verses. The terms following the opening phrase in 6:2 all confirm that Jesus is dead and that he went among the dead. The terms following the opening phrase in 6:11 seem to have been deliberately chosen to close off such an interpretation in regard to Mary. We will now examine the verses in detail to compare what they say.

Jesus went 'down to his garden, to the beds of spices.' The reference to spices here is a prophetic indication of his death. The gospels of Mark, Luke and John all speak of the women preparing spices and bringing them to honor the body of Jesus while he lay in the tomb. John explains that the use of spices in burial was customary among the Jews:

> They took the body of Jesus and bound it in linen cloths with the spices, following the Jewish burial custom.
> - John 19:40

This custom is evident in the account in 2 Chronicles of the burial of King Asa as far back as nine hundred years earlier:

> And Asa slept with his fathers ... He was buried ... with sweet odors and diverse kinds of spices ...   - 2 Chronicles 16:13,14

What Jesus was doing while his body lay in the tomb is explained in what follows. It is clear that Jesus went down among the dead for a specific reason. He went down 'to pasture his flock on the grass.' The pasturing of sheep is understood throughout Scripture as the preaching of the word of God to the people of God. This is what Jesus was doing when, in the words of 1 Peter 3:19, 'he went to preach to the spirits in prison.

'And to gather lilies.' The lilies, throughout the Song of Songs, are the innocent, the 'white,' those who have been redeemed and purified. There are quite a few references to lilies in the Song of Songs in which they carry this sense. Mary herself is 'a lily among brambles' (2:2). The table of the Holy Eucharist is 'surrounded by lilies' (7:3). The Groom 'feeds among the lilies' or he 'pastors his flock among the lilies' (2:16, 6:3).

So the purpose of Jesus' descent among the dead is clear. He is there to gather up his own and take them into his kingdom. This was prophesied in Song of Songs 6:2 several hundred years before it happened, and recounted in 1 Peter 3 and 4 after it happened.

Is something similar, or comparable, recorded of Mary in Verse 6:11? If it is then we have a reference to the Dormition in the Song of Songs. If not then so far as I can see, the Song of Songs contains no such reference.

In 6:11 Mary describes herself as going down 'to the nut orchard' or 'the garden of nuts.' I can find nothing in Scripture to suggest that nuts had any association with burial or the rituals of respect for the dead. One would have to stretch the meanings of the terms too far to see any parallel between this and Jesus going 'down to the beds of spices.'

Her purpose in going to the garden is 'to see the fresh shoots of the valley, to see if the vines were budding, and the pomegranate trees coming into flower.' These terms all refer to fresh growth. They run counter to any idea that Mary was going into the realms of the dead.

The souls of the dead in Purgatory can hardly be described as 'fresh shoots.' They are souls already saved, waiting in heaven's antechamber as their spiritual maturation is completed, until they have been wholly purified and ready for the fullness of life in heaven. These are not vines on the point of budding, or pomegranate trees on the point of coming to flower.

The verse reads more like a description of Mary going to her usual activities in the church community of the apostle John, with whom she shared a home. She was going to pray with and encourage the catechumens or the newly baptized, and to delight in seeing the first fruits of the Gospel becoming visible in them. It is possible she was going to visit the church in or near Jerusalem, though there is no evidence for that in the text.

The passage is one of a number of garden references in the Book, all of them alluding to the garden of the church in general. Mary was a gardener from her earliest childhood. As she declared to the elder virgins in the Temple when they looked critically at her dark skin coloring:

> "They made me the keeper of the vineyards."
> - Song of Songs 1:6

Nothing came more naturally to her as a little girl than to go out into her gardens to see if they were budding and the early flowers were appearing. We can only imagine the glory she gave to God and the joy she took in seeing her work in the gardens bear fruit, and her delight in bringing the fruits to the members of her family. The visits to gardens referred to in the Song of Songs came to symbolize her later eagerness to see the grace of God flowering in the church of which she would become the Queen and Mother.

> Come, my love,
>
> let us go into the fields,
>
> let us spend the night in the villages,
>
> in the early morning let us go to the vineyards.
>
> We will see if the vines are opening,
>
> if their blossoms are budding,
>
> if the pomegranates bud forth.
>
> - Song of Songs 7:12,13

The references here are to the beginnings of new life in the church in general, just as in 6:11.

At the end of the Song of Songs, in the second last verse, the Holy Spirit addresses Mary as the one who dwells in the gardens, and he calls upon her both to speak to the church and to pray to him:

> You that dwell in the gardens,
>
> my companions listen for your voice;
>
> cause me to hear it.
>
> - Song of Songs 8:13

Mary's work as a 'gardener' comes to its full fruition after her Assumption, after Jesus placed her as Mother and Queen of his entire kingdom, with full responsibility for its growth as its heavenly 'gardener.' She does this in union with the Holy Spirit. She expresses this with incomparable beauty in these words:

> Awake, O north wind,
> and come, wind of the south;
> breathe over my garden,
> to spread its sweet smell around.
> Let my beloved come into his garden,
> and eat its most exquisite fruits.
> - Song of Songs 4:16

These words are spoken by Mary to the Holy Spirit. The Holy Spirit responds:

> I come into my garden,
> my sister, my bride;
> I pick my myrrh and my balsam,
> I eat my honey and my honeycomb,
> I drink my wine and my milk
> - Song of Songs 5:1

The voice then addresses a larger audience which includes the entire church:

> Eat, friends, and drink;
> drink deeply, O dearest friends.
>
> Song of Songs 5:1

So when Mary goes down into the garden of nuts to see the fresh shoots growing, we are on familiar territory. Her instincts from her earliest childhood have been the instincts of a gardener. Her instincts in heaven as the Queen and Mother of the entire kingdom of her Son are the instincts of a gardener. And her instincts in the closing hours of her earthly life are those of a gardener. Her last activity in her earthly life is to go to look at the fresh growth in the life of new Christians in the garden of the very early church.

While the opening reference in verse 6:11 to going down to a garden, and the positioning of the verse immediately before the text which I read as a description of the Assumption, might make it momentarily attractive to read 6:11 as an allusion to a death and to a descent of her spirit among the dead, I believe the terms themselves don't support this interpretation. In fact I believe the terms of 6:11

are deliberately chosen to contrast with the terms of 6:2 rather than to conform to them.

There would be a further problem in any suggestion that Mary descended among the souls in Purgatory to encourage them and to rejoice in their growth. It would introduce a wholly new doctrine, one which has not been heard of throughout the two thousand year history of the church so far. It would be a novelty, the term sometimes used to characterize unsound ideas.

Dormition doctrine sees Mary being taken up into heaven by her Son shortly after her death. The idea doesn't seem to have occurred to anyone that she might have descended among the souls in Purgatory in the time between her death and her Assumption to mirror what Jesus did in the time between his death and Resurrection.

And a further problem: The narration of her activity in the garden in 6:11 runs continuously into the description of her Assumption in 6:12 via the expression, 'Before ever I was aware.' This expression tells us that the events in 6:12 and 7:1 began suddenly while she was in a garden to see if the new buds were coming forth. If that garden were Purgatory, then it would follow that the Assumption occurred in Purgatory. It didn't, of course. It occurred where her body was at the time, here on earth.

Someone will accuse me of setting up a straw man here. I admit that I am trying to resolve a problem of my own making, a problem that no doubt is meaningless for those who do not share my interpretations of the Marian references in the Song of Songs. My problem only arises because I regard Song of Songs 6:12 and 7:1 as a condensed prophetic description of Mary's Assumption; and for the sake of objectivity and truth I would like to be certain that Verse 6:11 does not support the view that she died first before I dismiss such a reading of it.

My conclusion is that Verse 6:11 gives no support to the view that Mary died before she was assumed. I believe that can be stated with certainty. In fact I believe that it gives support to the opposite view, that she was taken up while still alive.

Verse 8:5 is an often quoted reference to the Assumption:

> Who is this coming up from the desert
> leaning on her beloved?
> I raised you up under the apple tree
> there where your mother conceived you,
> there where she who conceived you
> brought you forth.
>
> - Song of Songs 8:5

This verse brings the Assumption together with the Immaculate Conception beautifully. The two doctrines are intimately linked, as we have noted before. Mary is seen 'coming up from the desert, leaning on her beloved,' after being 'raised up' by him 'under the apple tree,' which symbolizes the Cross.

The Cross, the 'apple tree' is the cause of both the Immaculate Conception and the Assumption, as was taught by the theologian Duns Scotus, and later by the teaching office of the Church.

The twin doctrines of the Assumption and the Immaculate Conception had been stated side by side in the Song of Songs 8:5 many centuries before either Duns Scotus or Pope Pius IX lived. God the Holy Spirit grasps the whole of time and everything that happens in time in a single moment. His knowledge is all encompassing. It is very easy for him to prophetically describe the things to come, as he does here, referring to her who comes up from the desert into heaven by the power given to her by her Son, who raised her up by the power of his Cross, under which she stood with him so steadfastly, so faithfully, during his terrible hours.

There is no indication in 8:5 that Mary died before she came up from the desert leaning on her beloved. The text switches abruptly to the account of her Assumption without any hint of a death preceding it.

The conclusion cannot be avoided: Mary's death is not indicated anywhere in the Song of Songs. Every one of the Church's doctrines concerning Mary receives prophetic support in the Song of Songs, most of them in several passages as we've seen in the previous chapter. There are passages in the Song of Songs which support both those doctrines which have been defined and those which are held by the Church without being formally defined. But the belief that Mary died before being assumed is not supported in any passage in the Song of Songs.

That there is no reference to the death of Mary in the Song of Songs is, in my opinion, an important piece of evidence in support of the view that she didn't die. It doesn't amount to compelling evidence; it doesn't amount to conclusive proof; but it does amount to strong support for the view that she didn't die.

IN THE MOMENTS BEFORE HER ASSUMPTION

We explored Verse 6:11 of the Song of Songs in the last chapter and concluded that it does not contain any indication that Mary died or spent time among the dead. We will now further explore what it does tell us about the circumstances of Mary's Assumption, linking it with what I think is the account of the Assumption that follows.

> I went down into the garden of nuts
> to see the fresh shoots of the valley,
> to see if the vines budded
> and the pomegranate trees
> were coming into flower.
> Before ever I was aware
> my desire had hurled me
> onto the chariots of Amminadib.
>   - Song of Songs 6:11,6:12

We began to consider in the previous chapter whether these two events – Mary going into the garden of the very early church to see its new growth, and Mary being thrown into the 'chariots,' ie, being taken up like Elijah – follow each other in an immediate sequence, or whether they are unrelated events. The Song of Songs does not always narrate events in time sequence. Sometimes it does, but it frequently makes abrupt changes between events and themes, and we would become very confused if we mistakenly read the text as a continuous sequential narrative from beginning to end.

In the case of Verses 6:11 and 6:12, the expression 'before ever I was aware' is conjunctive. It tells us that the narration following continues from the verse before. A story would not normally begin with, 'Before ever I was aware.' Where this phrase occurs, its context has already been set in the narration and it links what went before with what comes after.

So, if I am correct in my view that Verses 6:12 and 7:1 are a condensed prophetic account of Mary's Assumption, then we know that Verse 6:11 tells us what Mary was doing immediately before she was assumed. We know it because of that phrase, 'before ever I was aware.'

She was spending time with new Christians, observing their growth in the Spirit, rejoicing in the gifts God was lavishing on them by virtue of their faith in Christ.

Where was she doing this? We don't know. It may have been with the Christians of St John's church in Ephesus. Or she may have gone down to Jerusalem and met some of the apostles there.

As the Jerusalem church was probably the most mature church because it was there that the church was founded, it might be the less likely location for 'fresh shoots,' 'budding vines' and 'pomegranates coming into flower.' On the other hand, so many of the important events in salvation history took place in or near Jerusalem, and Mary herself returned frequently to Jerusalem throughout her life, that Jerusalem may well have been the place in which the Assumption took place.

We don't know the location, but it is clear that immediately before her Assumption she was with a group of new Christians in the very early church.

All of a sudden, 'before ever she was aware,' she was taken up. And her going up clearly caused a commotion among the disciples she was spending time with. Like the guests at weddings, they set up a cry:

> "Return, return O Shulamite!
> Return, return, that we may look upon you!"
> - Song of Songs 7:1

Like the fifty prophets who stood at a distance looking while Elijah was taken up, they didn't want to let her go. They didn't want her to leave them. They wanted her to come back.

Like the disciples who looked up after Jesus ascended, and continued looking up even after he had disappeared, they kept looking in the hope of catching one more glimpse of Mary even after she had been taken out of their sight.

Then the more mature voice spoke, with both a challenge and a resolution, a reason for hope. Elisha told the fifty prophets not to go looking for Elijah; Elisha had already been given a double share in his spirit. The two angels challenged the disciples after Jesus had been taken up: "Why do you stand there looking up? He will come back the same way he left you."

In the Song of Songs the Bridegroom asks a similar question: "Why do you look at the Shulamite?" The resolution in Mary's case is not that someone else has been given a share in her spirit, or that she will come back at some time in the future.

No. The resolution proposed in 7:1 by the Bridegroom is different: She hasn't really left you at all. "She dances between two armies." Yes, she has just been taken up to heaven. No, she has not ceased to be with the church here on earth, and she never will cease to be with us. She will always be fair as the moon, bright as the sun, and terrible as an army with banners. She will always bring the light and the power of heaven down to earth; and she will always be at work in her 'garden,' bringing her struggling, suffering, sinful children on earth through conversion to the fullness of the life God has destined for them in heaven.

THE ENMITY

In Chapter 3 of Genesis God prophesies a deep and long standing enmity that will last throughout history:

> "I will put enmity between you and the woman, and between your seed and her seed."
> - Genesis 3:15

St Louis Marie De Montfort comments on this enmity:

> The most fearful enemy that God has set up against the devil is Mary, his holy Mother ... He gave her such a hatred for his accursed enemy, such ingenuity in exposing the wickedness of the ancient serpent and such power to defeat, overthrow and crush this proud rebel, that Satan fears her not only more than angels and men but in a certain sense more than God himself.
> - TTD 52

This does not mean that Mary is more powerful than God. She has all her power from God. De Montfort explains:

> This ... simply means that Satan, being so proud, suffers infinitely more in being vanquished and punished by a lowly and humble servant of God, for her humility humiliates him more than the power of God.
>
> - TTD 52

We are not called to be neutral in the spiritual warfare. If we do not make our decision to line up with Christ, Satan will make the decision for us and line us up with himself. The enmity is between Satan and his offspring on one side, and Mary and her offspring on the other. Her offspring is Christ, and all those who believe in him.

We are called upon to follow Mary in hating Satan and his wicked angels. We are to give them no quarter. At our baptism we were asked, 'Do you renounce Satan? And all his works? And all his empty promises?'

The answer in each case is a resounding, 'I do!'

We are recommended to renew our baptismal promises frequently and to join Mary in utterly rejecting Satan and all his works.

Mary's hostility to Satan and all his insidious works is total hostility, total enmity.

Her victory over him is likewise total victory, given to her by God from the first moment of her existence.

Satan never gained any victory over Mary, not even the tiniest. The power the Mother of God has been given over God's greatest enemy is totally effective power. There is no breach in it. God's greatest creature has not been defeated by God's greatest enemy. That is why so many Christians instinctively recoil from any suggestion that she died. Any idea that Mary was overpowered by any of the works of the devil is repugnant.

We are allowed to believe in the Dormition, and I raise no protest against that permission. At the same time I am glad that we are also allowed to believe that Mary was assumed into heaven without tasting death.

THE APPARITIONS and REVELATION 12

The warfare between Mary and the dragon is described dramatically in Revelation 12. It is warfare to the death. The dragon fights with arrogance and showmanship and he gains a huge army of followers. He knows how to make his followers look good in this world. He knows how to promote them.

He is the 'busy trader' of Ezekiel 28:16. He uses all forms of hierarchy to make deals and get his people into the positions in which they can help his vile cause. He gets the great onto his side, the winners according to the standards of this world.

Arrogance is his hallmark. He has 'a mouth full of boasting' (Daniel 7:8 and Jude v.16).

Mary's strategy in the warfare is the opposite of all this; it is humble and subtle. She takes refuge in 'the desert' of the insignificant, the unimportant in the eyes of the world, the lowly, 'the things that are not' as St Paul expressed it (1 Corinthians 1:28).

The dragon will appear to win. He will appear to get the whole world onto his side. Then, when all seems lost, Mary will defeat him with her 'heel,' the great army of the insignificant ones who remain her children.

> And there appeared a great sign in heaven: a woman clothed with the sun, with the moon under her feet, and a crown of twelve stars on her head
>
> - Revelation 12:1

This is not a description of a defeated woman. It is not a description of a woman who has ever been overpowered by the dragon. It is not a description of a disembodied soul awaiting the resurrection of her body. It is a description of a woman who never tasted the defeat of death except in the death of her only Son, who underwent death in order to defeat it forever.

The warfare between Mary and the dragon has become particularly intense in recent centuries, and it continues to grow in intensity. Mary's public apparitions, in which she appeals for repentance and a return to acceptance of the Gospel in all its fullness, have been taking place with increasing frequency from the time of the apparitions at Lourdes in 1858.

We are not required to believe in her apparitions, even where they have received the approval of the Church, but we are strongly encouraged to do so.

As we mentioned earlier in regard to the Rosary, in all the public apparitions of Mary, I have never heard any declaration from her own lips that she died. There have been many affirmations of her Assumption, and of her Immaculate Conception, and of her Perpetual Virginity. I have heard of no affirmation by her that she died before she was assumed.

This does not prove the point. She may well want to show respect for both sides of the difference of view on the Dormition. That she never refers to her death, however, even as some of the greatest churchmen in history do, cannot be ignored. I think it is significant. It means that it is in no way displeasing to her when Christians believe that she was assumed while still alive.

Of course one could argue it the other way. She has not condemned the belief that she died, which must mean that she finds that view acceptable too.

It would be interesting to know if she herself 'expresses a view' one way or the other.

I hasten to clarify here that we need to be careful with private revelations, even where they have the seal of approval of the Church. The individual who receives such revelations needs to process and may even need to interpret what is heard, because what is spoken to the spirit is not always heard in clearly distinguishable words. The mind, which is fallible, shapes what is heard in accordance with its existing conceptions, and memory also can be less than totally reliable. It is possible too that Mary, not wishing to disturb the faith of Christians on matters not essential, speaks according to the understanding of the hearer.

With these caveats in mind, we can observe that Mary does seem to have said things which encourage a belief that she never died. To Fr Gobbi, for example, her chosen instrument in the spread of the Marian Movement of Priests, she confided that from the time of her birth her Heart was 'destined now never to stop beating' (MMP 550).

I don't wish to rely too heavily on this argument, but I think it right to bear in mind that Mary herself seems never to have alluded to her death, but does seem to have given cause to believe that she was assumed while still alive.

THE CHURCH OF ROME

There has been a gradual increase, over the course of the church's history, in the numbers of those who believe that Mary was taken up while she was still alive, that her Assumption means that she never died. This belief has been increasing primarily among the lay faithful, and primarily among western Catholics.

Is this point significant? Does it tell in favor of Mary's Assumption while she was alive? Is it not equally significant that eastern Christians, who after all were the first to give expression to a belief that Mary was assumed into heaven, have predominantly taken the view that she died before she was assumed?

The churches have different strengths. The great strength of the Church of Rome is, according to Scripture, its faith. Throughout church history Rome has led the way in sifting, in discerning, in judging, in defining the faith. It has done this not only for itself, but for all peoples 'throughout the whole world:'

> First, I give thanks to my God through Jesus Christ for you all, because your faith is spoken of throughout the whole world.   - Romans 1:8

If there has been a growing instinct among the members of the Church of Rome to honor Mary by affirming that she was assumed into heaven without experiencing death, that can be taken as strong support for the view that it happened like that.

There is a great reluctance among very many western Catholic Christians to admit that Mary died. The question comes up frequently, as we noted at the beginning of this work, and the questioners are typically puzzled to learn that they are expected to believe that she did die.

As we've also noted, western Catholic artists, seemingly without awareness that there is any issue to be discussed, have represented the Assumption as happening while Mary is in the midst of conversation with the members of the young church, who have been thrown suddenly into a kind of joyful consternation at her departure.

Their delineations of the Assumption conformed remarkably closely with the description of the Assumption in Song of Songs 6:11-7:1, as I understand this text. They probably didn't know it, but their understanding of the Assumption was strikingly similar to the description presented prophetically in Scripture.

That their instincts in this were so sound, as I believe they were, did not happen by chance. It happened because the Church of Rome has been given the gift by the Holy Spirit of true instincts in matters of faith for the benefit of the whole church.

THE THREE ASCENTS

Scripture contains three descriptions of persons going up to heaven from this earth. They are Elijah, Jesus, and Mary.

We've compared the scriptural accounts of the taking up of Elijah and the taking up of Mary. In this chapter we take a closer look at the Ascension of Our Lord for comparison with the Assumption of Mary. Our Lord ascended by his own power, but a comparison might nevertheless be helpful because the biblical record of his Ascension shares some common features with the descriptions of the taking up both of Mary and of Elijah.

We can remind ourselves of the common features here:

- In each case the person went up from earth to heaven in the presence of other believers.

- In each case, those other believers were reluctant to lose the person going up. There was a protest in some form, albeit a silent protest in the case of the Ascension of Jesus.

- A senior voice spoke words of gentle reprimand, telling the people left behind to get over it.

- The same voice pointed to compensatory factors, in one way or another telling them that they haven't really lost the person who went up, or at least that his spirit is still with them, or that they will see the person again.

The Ascension of Jesus is described by Luke in the opening chapter of Acts:

> When they had come together they asked him, "Lord, will you at this time restore the kingdom to Israel?" He replied, "It is not for you to know the times or the seasons which the Father has decided by his own authority, but you will receive power when the Holy Spirit comes upon you; and you will be my witnesses both in Jerusalem and throughout Judea, and in Samaria, and to the uttermost parts of the earth." And when he had said these things, while they looked, he was taken up, and a cloud received him out of their sight. And while they looked steadfastly toward heaven as he went up, two men stood by them in white apparel; and they said, "Men of Galilee, why are you standing gazing up into heaven? This same Jesus who has been taken up from you into heaven will come back in the same way as you have seen him go into heaven."
>
> - Acts 1:6-11

Though there are significant differences between the events recorded here and the events indicated in the Song of Songs 6:11-7:1, we can also see emerging the common patterns that we have noted above.

Jesus had already died and risen when he ascended. Mary, in my view, had not. However, Jesus had already been spending time with the disciples over a period of forty days, so his departure still affected them. They stood looking up as though reluctant to lose sight of him.

The description of the Ascension is much more specific and detailed than the allusive sketch of Mary's Assumption in the Song of Songs. 'He was taken up,' it is stated simply in Acts 1:9. The reference in Song of Songs 6:11 to 'the Chariots of Amminadib' is a much more allusive, much less explicit reference to the Assumption.

The apostles were present at Jesus' Ascension. There were also disciples present at Mary's Assumption, but we are not sure which disciples. There may have been apostles present. She was visiting the 'fresh shoots,' to see the early fruits in the garden of the church, suggesting that most if not all of the disciples present were new Christians.

Jesus spoke with authority to the disciples and gave them, and us, clear and reassuring instructions in the moments before he went up. These final, departing words prepared the disciples for separation. There is no record of Mary saying anything at her Assumption, and her going up took everyone by surprise and created commotion. In each case, the disciples present were deeply impressed at what they saw. At the same time there is a strong contrast between the calm, the silence, the equanimity among the disciples at Jesus' Ascension, and the abruptness of Mary's Assumption and the almost raucous reaction of those who were with her.

The seniors speaking to the disciples immediately after the Ascension were the two angels. The senior speaking to the disciples at the Assumption was Our Lord.

The initial messages of the senior persons are remarkably similar. The two angels challenged the apostles with: "Why do you stand there looking up." The Groom in the Song of Songs says: "Why do you look at the Shulamite?

The resolution is different in each case. The two angels assure the apostles that there is no point in looking up, because he will return in the same way as he left, with the hint that in the meantime there is work to do. Our Lord assures the disciples, and us, that Mary has not really left them, she is only 'dancing between two armies.' She has been taken to heaven, yes, but no, she hasn't left us on earth. She will always be with us.

Perhaps we need to add the final words of Jesus in Matthew: "And behold I am with you always, even to the close of the age" (Matthew 28:20). Jesus will always be with us too. The departing message of Jesus regarding himself is similar to the reassurance he gave to the disciples at Mary's Assumption, 'she dances between two armies.' She hasn't left you, and neither have I. We will be with our people the church until the end.

MATURING IN PRAISE

The history of the praises of Mary has been progressive. The Church has always given her high praises, and the degree of her praises has been ascending, throughout church history.

From earliest times she was acknowledged to be free of actual sin, but not of the original sin of Adam which we all contract at our conception. The idea that she was free of original sin, the idea of the Immaculate Conception, was very slow in developing. St Augustine believed she became free of the sin of Adam at or some time before her birth, but not from her earliest beginning. St Bernard, who was a pioneer in devotion to Mary, held a similar view, as did St Bonaventure and St Thomas Aquinas.

Sometime around the year 400 A.D. it began to dawn on people that Mary was not only the Mother of the man Jesus. She was the Mother of the Person, the Son of God. The question arose in connection with a saying that had become popular in some parts of the church: 'A Person of the Trinity died on the Cross.' Church authorities were called on to correct this idea, but instead of correcting it, they declared that it is true. A Person of the Trinity did indeed die on the Cross, just as a Person of the Trinity inhabited the womb of the Blessed Virgin for nine months. The doctrine of Mary

Mother of God was declared as dogma, a necessary part of our faith, at the Council of Ephesus in 431 A.D.

But for reasons we do not wholly understand, the Church took a much longer time to define the doctrine of the Immaculate Conception as part of our faith. And because it is intimately bound up with the doctrine of the Immaculate Conception, the doctrine of the Assumption took even longer to be confirmed in definitive Church teaching.

The Assumption was known about much earlier. It was established as a feast in the western Church around the year 800 A.D. It was defined as a doctrine of the faith in 1950.

We can validly ask the question whether the doctrine might be further developed as we further develop our capacity to praise God's greatest creature, Mary.

> The whole world is filled with her glory ... and yet in truth we must still say with the saints: *De Mariae numquam satis*: We still have not praised, exalted, honored, loved and served Mary adequately. She is worthy of even more praise, respect, love and service.
> - TTD9,10

Are we being called to give greater glory to the Mother of the Church by affirming that she was taken up like Elijah, while still alive? Is this a direction the Church is called to take? Did St Epiphanius instinctively point the direction toward which the church has been slowly led over many centuries?

> And if I should say anything more in her praise, she is like Elijah, who was ... taken up and has not seen death.

It is not for me to tell the Church what doctrines to teach. I only give expression to an opinion: that we have been gradually moving in the direction of affirming her Assumption while alive. I expect we will one day be able to declare with complete confidence that she was taken up in the manner of Elijah rather than Moses.

CONCLUSION

At the end of this short work we are not able to answer our question with absolute certainty. The Church has pronounced definitively that Mary was assumed into heaven at the end of her earthly life. The Church has not pronounced on whether she died before she was taken up. Perhaps she never will pronounce definitively on this question, and the question will only be answered for us in heaven.

In the meantime it is legitimate to believe either way. We will not lose the faith of the apostles either by believing that Mary was assumed shortly after dying, or by believing that she was assumed without dying.

The arguments in favor of the Dormition are strong and impressive. The churchmen who first believed in Mary's Assumption were convinced that she died first. The Assumption was their answer to the question, What happened her after she died?

And the great majority of senior churchmen throughout the history of the church have taken the view that she died first. These include recent popes, including one who has been canonized, Pope St John Paul II. They even include the pope who defined the Assumption as dogma, Pope Pius XII. The adherence of such persons to the teaching of the

Dormition makes it impossible to deny that this teaching is still respectable.

Some of the saints most devoted to Mary have taken the same view. These include St Bonaventure and St Alphonsus Liguori, who are surely among the most eloquent devotees of Mary who ever lived. If these believed in Mary's Dormition, then it cannot be asserted that this teaching lacks good credentials. On the contrary, its credentials are outstanding.

The other argument in favor of the Dormition has very strong support in Scripture. This is the argument that the death of Christ has altered the language we use about death, which cannot now be seen simply as a defeat or a curse, because death has become the gateway through which we unite ourselves with Christ and are lifted up into his Resurrection.

'Blessed are the dead who die in the Lord henceforth.' Doesn't this mean that there is no longer any reason to resist the idea that Mary died?

We have countered this by asserting that Mary did indeed die. She was united with her Son, not in a further death of her own, but in his own death when she suffered alongside him all the way to Calvary and the piercing of his side with the sword of Longinus. The sword that pierced Mary's Heart was driven into the Heart of Jesus, causing her far deeper pain than any sword that could ever have been driven into her own.

In our short work we've traced, very sketchily and unprofessionally, the history of the development of the doctrine of the Assumption of Mary. We've seen that its development was remarkably gradual, as was the development of the doctrine of the Immaculate Conception. It passed through a number of phases, each phase lasting centuries.

In the first three centuries there are no written records of the end of Mary's life at all. Then there begin to appear a number of written accounts of her Dormition and her Assumption in the presence of the apostles. These records contain detail that can be regarded as fanciful, they are published anonymously or pseudonymously, and they are generally not well received by Church authorities.

Centuries ahead of his time, in the 370s, St Epiphanius, in a long book defending Christian doctrine against heresies, expressed an intuition, a hope, which at the time he did not feel free to declare with anything like certainty, that Mary was taken up to heaven like Elijah, without seeing death. It was more than a thousand years before this idea found public expression again.

In the late 700s the Assumption was instituted as a Feast in the western Church calendar, and before long its name was changed from the Dormition of Mary to the Assumption of Mary. The shift in emphasis had begun. It continued in the centuries up to about the year 1500, when in the references to the end of Mary's life in the Mass, mention of her death was gradually phased out, to be replaced by mention of her resurrection and Assumption.

By around the year 1500, as we can see from the works of artists on the subject of the Assumption, the popular imagination had already accepted the idea of Mary being taken up without dying. The idea must also have been at least tolerated by some churchmen, because these works of art were commissioned for use in churches.

The idea of Assumption without death received historic impetus in 1854, when Pope Pius IX defined the Immaculate Conception of Mary. This definition disabled a primary argument in favor of the death of Mary, and from that time the question of whether she died has been a frequent topic in Mariology.

It is probably still true to say that belief in Mary's Assumption without death is more common among lay Christians than among churchmen. A trend has been established nonetheless, not in any way impeded by the fact that Mary herself, in her recognized apparitions in recent centuries, has referred many times to her Assumption but has never referred to her death.

We looked at the question which is often asked: If Mary did die, who was the agent of her death? Which destroyer did God release against her? We found that, because of her freedom from all trace of sin, including the original sin passed down from Adam and Eve, there was no agent of death. No destroyer was released against her.

We addressed the argument that she died in the ordinary course of 'nature,' and found this argument wanting in the light of Scripture. The argument is often pressed, that our bodies are naturally designed to decay like the bodies of animals and plants; that animals and plants died a natural death before Adam sinned, and continue to die a natural death afterwards; and that there is no reason to suppose that humans were not always destined to end their lives in the same 'natural' way as plants and animals.

Scripture answers this argument in Genesis Chapters 2 and 3. In the beginning, when God placed our first parents in the Garden of Eden, the tree of life was in the middle of the garden alongside the tree of the knowledge of good and evil. Adam and Eve were free to eat of the fruit of the tree of life and so live forever before they ate of the tree of the knowledge of good and evil. They continued to enjoy that freedom as long as they obeyed the commandment by refraining from eating the fruit of the tree of the knowledge of good and evil. They were only expelled and cut off from access to the tree of life after they had sinned by eating of the fruit of the tree of the knowledge of good and evil.

The Bible shows us what would have happened to all of us if we had not been infected with sin. Enoch and Elijah, when they reached the end of their earthly lives, did not die a 'natural' death; they were taken up by God because they had walked with him and pleased him during their lives. Scripture tells us without any ambiguity that this is how they finished their course on this earth. No reason can be found to deny that the same happened to the Mother of God.

We have examined Scripture to see if we can find any account of the Assumption of Mary in any part of it. There are a number of scriptures in the Old and New Testaments which indicate that Mary was assumed body and soul into heaven, or that show her in heaven in her glorified body (Psalm 45 and Revelation 12 for example); but can we find any passage in Scripture in which the event itself is described?

I take the view that the event is described prophetically in the Song of Songs 6:11-7:1. We compared this text with the descriptions of the assumption of Elijah and of the Ascension of Our Lord, and found sufficient common features to justify interpreting the text in the Song of Songs as a description of Mary's Assumption.

We then examined verse 6:11 of the Song of Songs to see if it gives us any clues as to what Mary's circumstances were immediately before she was assumed. We considered at length whether it could be read as an indication that she had died and gone down among the souls in purgatory, as Jesus went among the souls of the redeemed dead in between his death and his Resurrection. We compared verse 6:11 with verse 6:2 for this purpose.

We found the terms of verse 6:2 different from the terms of verse 6:11. While 6:2 is a clear reference to Jesus' descent among the dead, 6:11 does not indicate that Mary did something comparable before her Assumption.

We ascertained that verse 6:11 does indeed tell us what Mary was doing immediately before she was assumed. It becomes clear when we notice the expression at the beginning of verse 6:12, 'Before ever I was aware,' which establishes that 6:11 is joined with 6:12-7:1 in a continuous narrative. From this we know that immediately before her Assumption, Mary was spending time with a group of recently converted Christians. This is consistent with the expressions of consternation in 7:1 which accompany her being taken up. "Return, return O Shulamite!/Return, return that we may look upon you!"

This description in the Song of Songs is remarkably similar to the view of the Assumption of Mary which has taken hold in the popular imagination of the western Catholic church, as expressed in works of art such as Titian's Assumption, painted around 1517 A.D. Whether Titian consciously modeled his painting on this text from the Song of Songs, I have no way of knowing. It is very likely that he had no idea that his painting was based on a scriptural model at all, which makes it all the more remarkable to see the similarity between his visual portrayal and the biblical description.

I am well aware that not everyone will agree with my interpretation of the Song of Songs 6:11-7:1. Some will see it as eccentric and arbitrary, an attempt to fit the word of God around my existing conceptions rather than to fit my conceptions around the word of God. Others will tell me I am not paying enough attention to scholarship and that if scholars cannot determine what the human author meant by this biblical text, I have no business pretending to determine it from a perspective which is not scholarly.

I understand these arguments, and reply that it is not wrong to seek agreement between what the Holy Spirit has told us in Scripture and what he has told us in Sacred Tradition. The Holy Spirit does not contradict himself. I did not learn about the Assumption of Mary by plucking the idea out of the air. I learned it from the definitive teaching of the Catholic Church. If we can see a scripture or scriptures which can reasonable be interpreted as describing the event and confirming the authoritative teaching, I see no good reason to call that an eccentric or arbitrary practice.

As to scholarship, I emphasize that scholarship is very useful and can be very valuable. It helps us to understand what the human author meant, speaking within his historical circumstances. Scholarship, however, should not be used to bind the Holy Spirit's hands, so to speak. The Holy Spirit frequently says things with multiple layers of meaning, as Jesus did in his parables. There are very many prophecies in Scripture the fullness of whose implications the human author at the time of his writing did not comprehend.

We are not thereby prohibited from asking the Holy Spirit what he meant by the words he caused to be written down. It is wholly legitimate to do so. It is wholly legitimate to revise our understanding of scriptural texts as the Holy Spirit leads us to grow in understanding. I believe it is wholly legitimate to read Song of Songs 6:11-7:1 as a description of the bodily Assumption of Mary even if the human author of these verses had no idea that this is what he was describing.

In the end, the question we set ourselves in this work cannot be answered definitively, at least not yet. I may be proved wrong, but I feel that the historic trend has already been set.

St Louis Marie De Montfort urged the church to greatly increase the praises it gives to Mary, as we have not yet learned to praise her enough. In doing this he gave expression to a godly instinct, because if God himself praises Mary as lavishly as he praises her in Scripture, it is surely right for the church to join him in the praises he gives to his greatest creature.

St Epiphanius, the saintly father and warrior against heresy, had an early intuition, when awareness of the place of Mary in God's plan was beginning to dawn in his church. That intuition may well provide a clue to one direction in which the praises of Mary are being led by the Holy Spirit. "And if I should say anything more in her praise," Epiphanius wrote, "she is like Elijah, who ... was taken up and has not seen death."

"If I should ..." At the time he wrote these words, St Epiphanius was unsure whether he should lift his praises of

Mary to such heights. He only felt free to give her this praise conditionally. He feared being condemned if he were to declare his intuition outright.

In our own time, there is no reason for such fear. The doctrine of the Assumption has been defined, and we are wholly free to take the position that St Epiphanius feared to take though he earnestly wanted to: that Mary, like Elijah, was assumed into heaven body and soul without having tasted death.

www.ingramcontent.com/pod-product-compliance
Lightning Source LLC
Chambersburg PA
CBHW031445040426
42444CB00007B/976